SOMETHING FOR 10:30

Involvement Cards for Social Skills

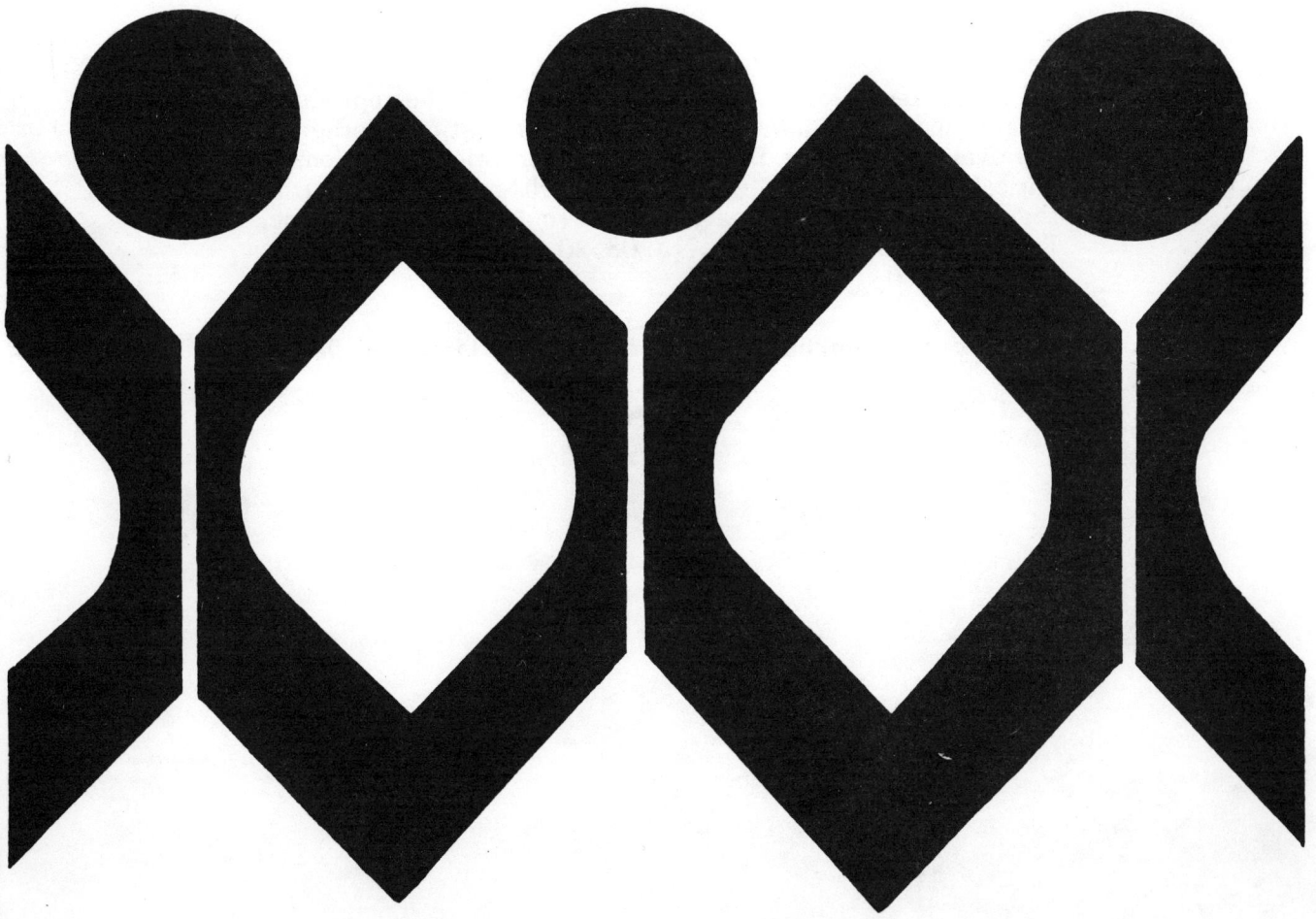

by amy maid and tim timmermann

First N.L. Associates, Inc. Edition 1987

Copyright ©1977 by Mandala

Library of Congress Cataloging in Publication Data

ISBN 0-8290-0353-3

Printed in the United States of America

The Whole Thing

> *"I am a part of all that I have met."* **Tennyson**

• Experience something (or someone). Look at it, touch it, really see what you are seeing. Share it with someone.

• Get together with one other person and talk about the things that influence YOU (people, places, things, or situations).

• Close your eyes — find your center and stay there for several minutes. In your journal record what comes to you while you are there. Tell someone about it.

• Graph yourself: Draw an outline of yourself on a piece of graph paper (work large). Using different colors, shade in the number of boxes that show how much of you is you, other people, places, things, etc. Make a key for your graph so that other people can "read" it.

• With another person, make a poster advertising this quotation.

• With three other people, discuss the following —

   → What happens to your experience once you've had it
   → What different things do people include as "experiences"
   → What similarities do you see in the collages you've done
   → How would someone who is older make their collage differently

• Make a word and/or picture collage of your last **4** years experience.

• With several of your classmates, plan an experience to be enacted before your entire class. Suggestions for the experience are:

quick non-related events	a formal reading	three minutes of silence
a comedy routine	singing a song	a mock murder

When the event is over, ask the class to tell you exactly what they saw happen. Try to see how different people see differently. Point out how people see what they want to see.

tomorrow & tomorrow &

tomorrow & tomorrow &....

TOMORROW AND TOMORROW AND TOMORROW . . . .

"One of these days is none of these days." **English proverb**

- In your journal, write a paragraph on your style of getting things done.
    - Are you more of a starter?
    - Are you more of a finisher?
    - Are you one who works better alone?
    - Are you one who works better with others?
    - Do you wait until the last minute?
    - Are you done before deadlines?
    - In what other ways do you describe your "doing personality?"

then *tomorrow* *NOW* *TODAY* *when* *Yesterday*

- With three others, brainstorm what you think the future will be like. Put your list on newsprint so others can add to it and react to yours. Take one of the items and write an essay on it. See if you can get your essay printed in the local paper.

- In your journal, list the things you put off doing. Answer the question "why" after each one.

- Put off doing the rest of this activity card for 25 minutes (check the time). Afterwards, describe to someone how you felt about putting it off. What did you do during your 25?

- DO SOMETHING that you've been putting off (RIGHT NOW!) Tell someone about it when you have finished.

- In a small group do some whips on the topics:

    My feelings when others are late . . . .
    I'm late when . . . .
    Something I avoid doing . . . .
    Ways to not put off doing things . . . .
    One of these days I'm going to . . . .

- Have a class discussion on "How important do you think it is to do things IMMEDIATELY?"

- Be alone for a few minutes. Relax and dream about the time of the day passing. How do you "see" time? Picture it. Tell someone what you saw in your dream.

what..?

WHAT ❓

〜〜〜〜〜〜〜〜〜〜〜〜〜〜〜

■ With three others, make a list of ways to show how you go about finding answers to questions. Present your list to your class.

■ Have a class discussion on uncertainty (not having answers).

■ Write a poem in which you ask some questions that you would like answered.

With two others, write some questions that you know don't have answers.
Example: Do you walk to school or carry your lunch? Why is it, when you walk into a room?

■ Have a discussion on how you feel about someone who "knows all the answers."

■ Pick **1** of the following statements and give a one-minute defense of it:

　☐ Beware of the knower in you who knows; to know a thing is not to have to experience it again

　☐ Imagination is more important than knowledge (Einstein)

　☐ Oftener than not, understanding gets the booby prize

　☐ Being right doesn't work

WHO KNOWS?

■ Find a way to prove that you are real. Keep hearing a voice saying, "prove it."

do it !

DO IT !!! ✓

"What we have to learn to do, we learn by doing."

✳Go to your school's library. Take out a "How-to-do-it" book. Read about how to do something. Do it! Describe your learning experience to another person.

✳Get the class's attention and ask — If seeing is believing, explain how believing is seeing.

✳Write yourself a note in your journal about something you want to learn to do in the next year. How will you be different after?

✳Tell someone about something you want to learn to do before you die, and why. Listen to what s/he has to say too.

✳THINK: What makes you want to do things? What makes you stay on the "sidelines?"

✳Journal activity: When it comes to learning something new, what things (both in and outside you) work for you and what things get in your way? Make two lists.

✳With the first grade teacher: make up a simple learning game for younger children (e.g. teaching rhyming words, addition facts, telling left from right). Try it out. Did it work? Why or why not? What did you learn by making up the game?

✳Make a list of the reasons people learn. Rank-order them three different ways.

✳Write about something you learned to do that changed your life.

✳Make a poster with the title: "No one can teach anything — we can only learn."

WHAT A BREAK....

WHAT A BREAK . . .

●●●

"It was not foolish/ of the car/ to smash the wall:
It was foolish/ of me to/ have had bad brakes."

●●●

●Class discussion: Guns don't kill people, people kill people
Who is responsible for your feelings?

●Make a "responsibility chain." List all the people (all things) that are responsible for you, and all the people (and things) that you are responsible for. Analyze your chain.

●Write an essay on "Why many people find it hard to be responsible for themselves and their actions."

●Write a fable called "The Beginning of Responsibility"

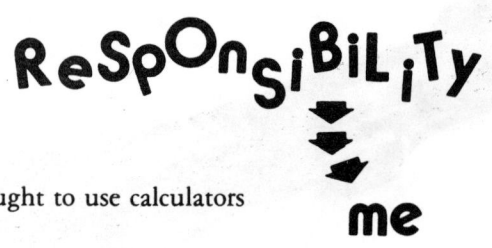

ReSPOnSiBiLiTy
↓↓
me

●TAKE A STAND on one of the following issues . . . . .
 Girls have the same amount of athletic ability as boys
 Children shouldn't be taught Math . . . they should be taught to use calculators
Make a poster expressing your point of view.

●In a small group make a list to define the word "responsibility"
Give examples of when you've noticed responsibility happening
Do the same thing for the word "blame"
Figure out some ways to dramatize the two words for your classmates.

●Alone activity: Close your eyes and begin to make a list of the things and places where you were responsible. When you think you have your list "see" some more. Reverse the scene and make yourself irresponsible. In your journal write about the difference.

●In you journal make a list of people who fit these categories:

Victim ▬ Persecutor ▬ Rescuer

●Victim is one who always feels someone is picking on them
●Rescuer is one who is always helping, making sure everything is going all right
●Persecutor is one who blames

See if you can find the times when these people play their roles. Watch for them and try not to play a role that keeps them in theirs. Example: When someone is blaming you don't be a victim.

DON'T LOSE THIS...

DON'T LOSE THIS . . . .

"There are defeats more triumphant than victories." **Montaigne**

• With three others make up a game in which nobody wins. Discuss whether this is possible to do. Describe to your class any problems you ran into.

• Do a class meeting — what does losing mean? What kinds of things do people lose?

• Interview several people on the question — "Is it possible to lose and still be a winner?" Present your information to the class.

• Discuss the popular saying — "It's not whether you win or lose, it's how you play the game."

• Interview some people (kids and adults) to find out the most "important" things people have won and lost. Evaluate the results.

• With two others discuss losing the following: (evaluate what has been lost and how the situation could be turned into a victory)

a $1 bet

a friend

a race

face

an elected office

a dream

integrity

• Write a proverb and make a poster about winning and/or losing.

• Close your eyes: Put the word "winning" on the back of your eye lids and wait to see what comes to you. Take what you get and share it with someone.

YOU'VE GOT TO START SOMEWHERE

DONT WALK

start

YOU'VE GOT TO START SOMEWHERE . . .

"Don't let life discourage you; everyone who got where he is had to begin where he was." Richard L Evans

► Where were you? Where are you at now? Where do you plan to be in the future? Draw a map of your life based on your answers.

► Journal activities:
Explain why it is sometimes hard to start things
How do you know when to "give up?" How do you know when to "go on?"
I was . . . now I am . . . (complete several of these sentences about you)

►"If you don't succeed at first, try, try again." What's the message? Draw a cartoon showing what it means.

► Class discussions:
The times when you get discouraged. Describe how you feel
Wherever you are is where you are — there is no past or future only the present
Your now is that you are where you were
Life is the way it is — you can't change now
Wherever you are is perfect
Don't change the world — change the way you look at the world
Stop trying and let go. Then "it" will happen

►Class project: Decide as a group a goal you would like to reach in the next four weeks. Do things like — —
▪ divide into things-to-be-done
▪ plan check points for week 1, 2, 3, and finish
evaluate:
•your style of cooperation/competition
•your effectiveness
•your final product with what you first expected
•what you did with people who didn't carry their share of the tasks

start

ACTING OUT

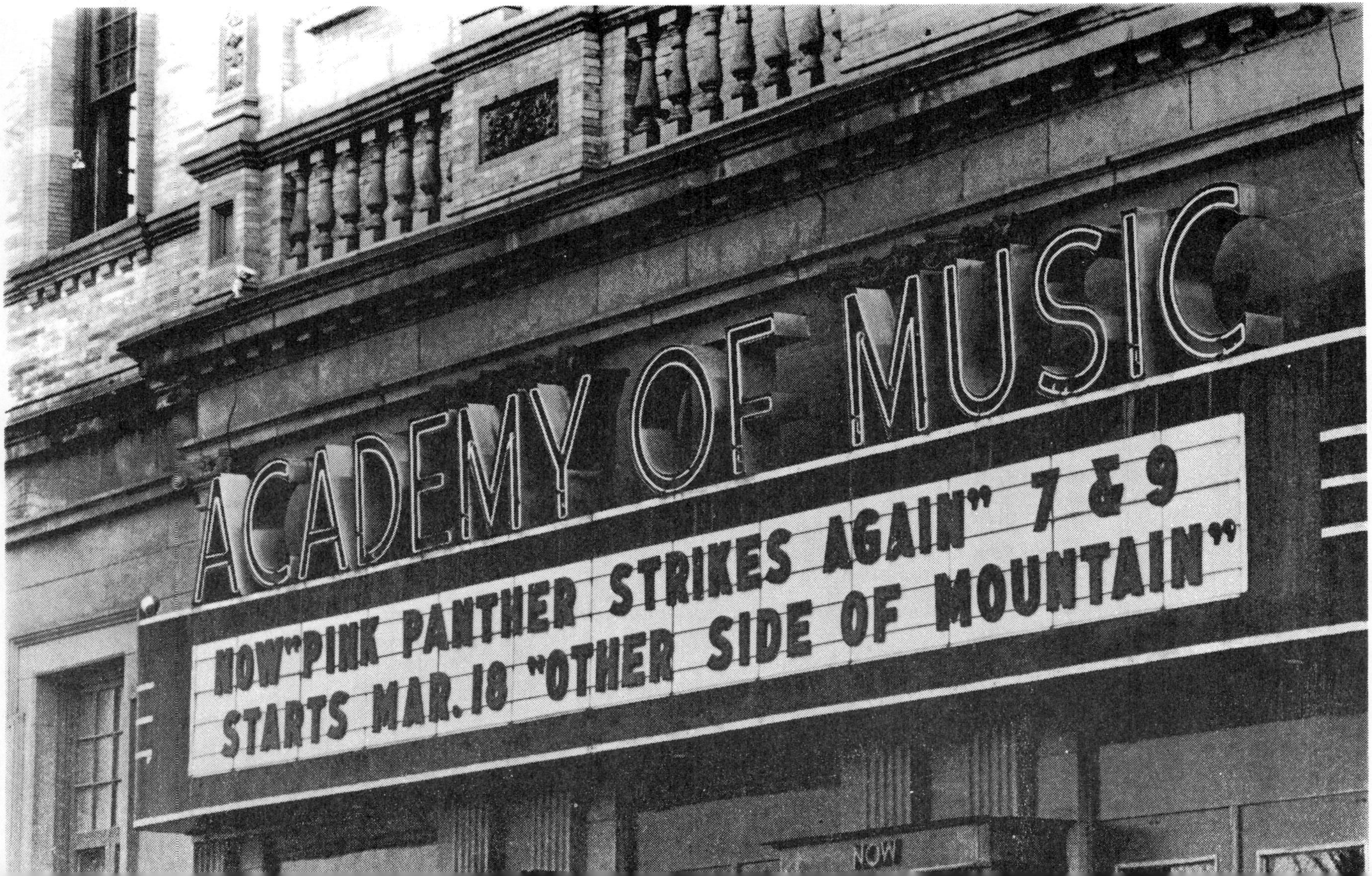
ACADEMY OF MUSIC
NOW "PINK PANTHER STRIKES AGAIN" 7 & 9
STARTS MAR. 18 "OTHER SIDE OF MOUNTAIN"
NOW

"It is by acts and not by ideas that people live." **Anatole France**

- Draw a picture of an idea turning into an action.

- Make a collage of your ideas. Try not to think about them — let them flow into your mind.

- Write a imaginary story or poem about an idea that gets lost . . . .

idea ↔ ACTION

- In a small group, discuss:
  ideas you live by
  hunches you've had about life
  actions speak louder than words
  when to act and when to think

- With three others do one of the following projects:
  Make up a cookbook on how to get ideas
  Write a play with the title:
  "If you act before you think you're . . ." or
  "If you think before you act you're . . ." Act it out for your class.

- Find some alone time:
  Close your eyes and relax for a few minutes. Count your breaths five times. In your mind's eyes see your ideas. Don't try to think — let your mind do what it does so well — think on its own. In your journal record your thoughts. Do this for the next five days. Are there any patterns or things you mind thinks often?

- Something to think about —
  If your mind thinks things by itself do you have to take responsibility for your thoughts?

RELATIONSHIPS

RELATIONSHIPS . . .

"Be slow in choosing a friend, slower in changing . . ." **Ben Franklin**

• Make a list of what you need a friend to be. In your journal, write why you think you need these things.

• Write the biography of your imaginary friend.

• In a group, discuss FRIENDSHIP and the following: obligation
honesty
trust
loyalty
disappointment
individuality

be a friend...

• Write a note to yourself about how you know when you have a friend.

• Friendship is a recipe made up of many different ingredients. In your journal, write your special recipe for friendship. After, trade recipes with someone else.

• Write **5** words that describe the qualities YOU look for in a friend.

• Fill in the blanks: I know a friendship is over when _____

Friendships end because _____

• In your journal, write about whether it is harder for you to make a friend or keep a friend.

• Find 1 or 2 people, compose, rehearse and present to the class some skits about "fictional friendships" like:

• Betty and Veronica   • Laverne and Shirley

• Fonzie and Ritchie   • _____ **?** and _____ **?**

how many?

HOW MANY????

"Man was endowed with two ears and one tongue, that he may listen more than speak."
Zeno of Citium

● Stay absolutely quiet for 5 minutes and LISTEN to the sounds around you. At the end of the 5 minutes, write about what you heard.

moo

● Draw a picture (or make a collage) of sounds.

hiss

● Do some whips on —
    Your feelings when people don't listen to you
    Times when you enjoy listening
    Something you wish you could hear

bang

clink

● In your journal —
    Record ten people you speak with often. Beside each name place an:

        L if the person listens more than speaks
        S if the person speaks more than listens
        IL if you listen to this person more than you speak
        IS if you speak to this person more than you listen

    What are some of the reasons for these kinds of relationships?

● Have a class meeting to diagnose your class as one which listens.
    Have all the students rank 0 - 10 its listening behavior.
                    0 - 10 its speaking behavior.
                0 = do not listen . . . 10 = super listeners
                0 = hesitate to speak . . . 10 = speak with no hesitation

● Have your classmates brainstorm the following —
    Reasons we value listening
    Reasons we value speaking

psst

tick tock

● With two others discuss —
    How you know you've been listened to
    Some people hear but don't listen

What's in a name?

"Every man has three names; one his father and mother gave him, one others call him, and one he acquires himself."

Investigate your name (first, middle, last). Find out what your names mean and if possible, why you were given your name.

sarah   diane   ed

•Choose another name for yourself. In your journal, write about your choice. Practice writing your "new" name.

nat   luke

•For a few hours, trade names with a classmate. After you've got your name back, discuss the experience with that person.

emily   linda   roger   wayne

•In a group, discuss: "Sticks and stones can break my bones but names can never hurt me"
How does a person acquire his/her names? Do these names stay the same throughout a person's life or do they change?

lorine   bob

•In your journal, write how you feel about the name you have. Which name are you most comfortable with? Proud of? Disappointed in?

david   sheryl   joel

•Copy 3 or 4 names out of a phone book (no one you know). Write a short description for each of the people on the list. How did you get the picture of these people in your mind? Why do you think you were able to write the descriptions? How do names influence the way you think about people? Discuss with your sharing-partner-for-the-day.

ann   suzi   jim

•What labels do you wear to show people who and what you are? Make a collage of labels that are YOU.

amy   gail

•Make word or picture drawings of: the way your parents see you
the way others see you
the way you see yourself

marilyn   lori   tim   barry

•Write your name, very large and very slowly in perfect penmanship; stay in touch with the feelings you get as you are doing this. Share the experience with someone.

Sounds Of Silence

THE SOUNDS OF SILENCE

"The cruelest lies are often told in silence." **Robert Louis Stevenson**

★ Write a poem about yourself — everything you say must be a lie.

★ As a class project: Find examples in our society that show how "we" feel about truth and lying. For example: The story of Pinnochio or the TV game show Truth or Consequences. Brainstorm with someone else.

★ With another person discuss: Is telling the truth the same as not lying?
　　　　　　　　Why people lie
　　　　　　　　How you know the truth
　　　　　　　　How silence is sometimes the same as lying

★ In your journal: Record some of your lies.
　　　　What kind do you remember?
　　　　Do you have any "left over" business with anyone?
　　　　What's it like to write down your lies?

Shh...

★ Write a fable called "The First Lie Ever . . ."

The Grass is

Always Greener

"He that has one eye is a prince among those that have none." Thomas Fuller M.D.

WANT WHAT YO !

- Write a story about how the saying "green with envy" got started.

- What would you put in the blank? "What you _____ is what you get."

- In a group discuss the following:

  How do you know when you are satisfied **?**

  Where do people get ideas to want things **?**

- Write a note to yourself about the things that you want that you don't already have.

- Draw some cartoons to show the differences between:

  admiration and envy ▬ hope and envy ▬ ambition and envy

- Next time you feel yourself experiencing envy, pay special attention to how you act and the things you say to yourself. Share these observations with someone else.

- Make 2 lists: "Things I envy in other people" and "Things other people might envy in me." When you finish, write one sentence about your lists.

getting things

auop

GETTING THINGS DONE . . .

●●

"The reward of a thing well done is to have done it" **Emerson**

●●

☆ List **5** words that describe the things you do whenever you feel proud.

☆ In a group, discuss the following:
- how is pride a reward?
- as people get older, do the rewards for doing things change?
- how you decide whether or not to do something
- where do rewards come from . . . are they self-created or other-created?

☆ In your journal tell which is easier for you: receiving a compliment or giving one.

☆ Make a poster advertising your accomplishments.

☆ Write **15** *different* ways to say, "well done!"

WOW!

☆ Make a list of rewards you'd like to receive. How do you go about getting them? (Make an entry in your journal).

●●

Somewhere

Over The Rainbow

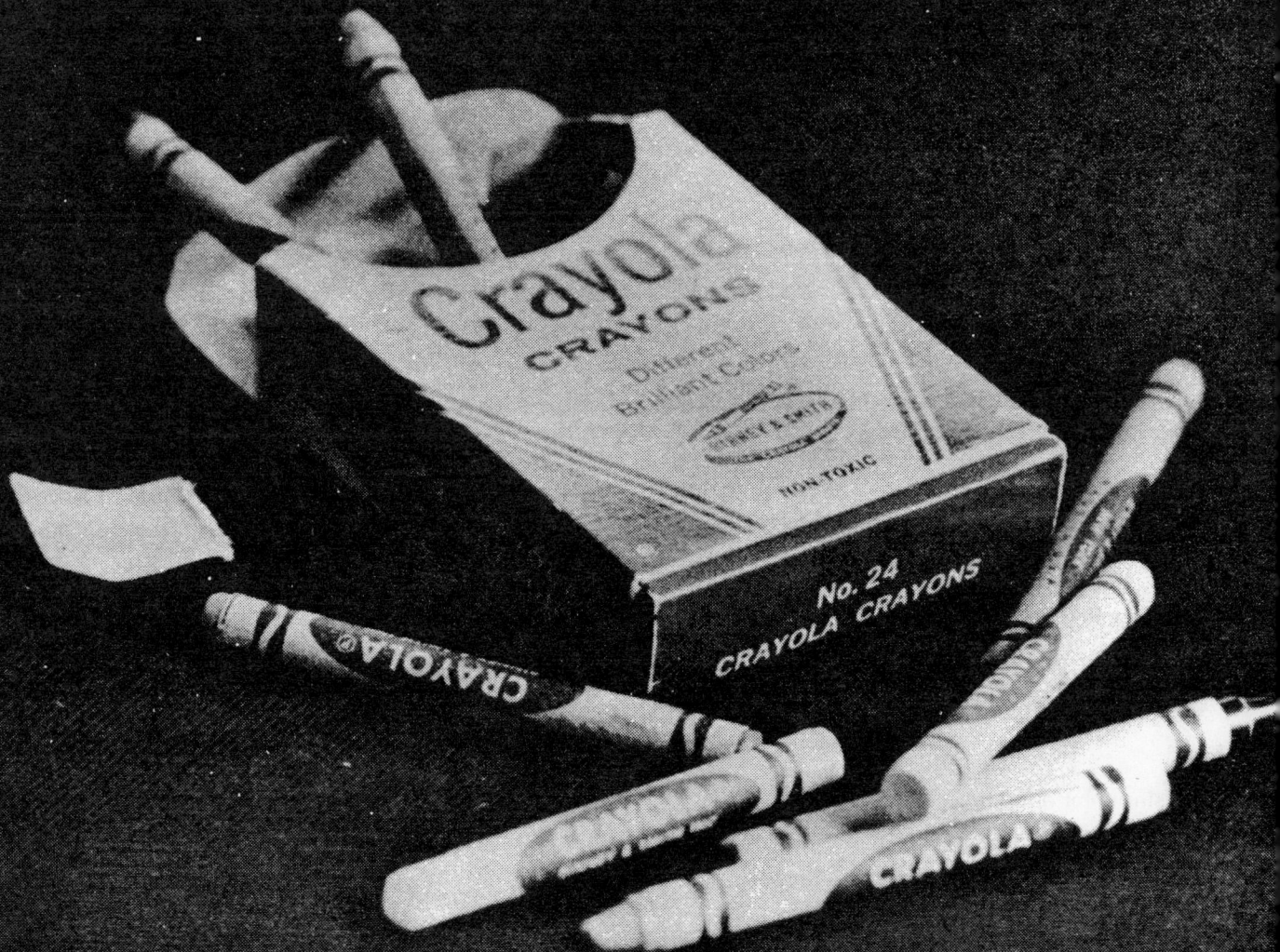

SOMEWHERE OVER THE RAINBOW

RED

"Colors speak all languages." Joseph Addison

◆◆◆◆◆◆◆◆◆◆◆◆◆◆◆◆◆◆◆◆◆◆◆◆

●Discuss with 2 or 3 people: how color influences feelings
how people share color
who colors belong to

●Close your eyes for a few seconds and put all your attention on: the colors of day/night and the colors of the seasons . . . can you pretend to be those colors for a little while? Describe what you see to your sharing-partner-for-the-day.

●In your journal, write down some of the things you say to yourself about the color of other people's skin and the color of your skin.

●Find one or two other people and act out what it feels like to be:
a primary color
a pastel color
a new box of crayons
a kaleidoscope
a rainbow

rouge

●Close your eyes: choose a color to see and watch it change behind your eyes. Write one sentence about your experience. Give it to your teacher.

●Make a color wheel of YOU.

ROJO

●Things that are colorless — draw one or two.

●Color something for someone (give it to that person).

●Using color *only*, draw:

quiet   truth   hope

loneliness   mystery   wealth

imagination   energy

excitement   depression

comedy   panic   ✱ Choose 6 from this list.

THE GOLDEN RULE

"If a man destroy the eye of another man, they shall destroy his eye." **Code of Hammurabi**

● Make up your own dictionary entry for: "getting even."

● Write one sentence that tells what you "get" when you get even.

● Physicalize JUSTICE. Do this with a partner.

● With 3 or 4 other people, brainstorm a definition for "fair" and then discuss:

Is the Code of Hammurabi fair?
Is revenge fair?
Is justice fair?

FAIR IS . . . *

● Ask some people to think about solving the problems of crime and punishment in this country . . . Publish the suggestions in a class information sheet or newsletter.

● Who was Hammurabi? Research, and choose a way to present what you have learned to the rest of your class (e.g. chart, poster, comic book, short report).

● With a partner, write a NEW and IMPROVED Code of Justice.

● Close your eyes for a moment and re-create a time when you were wronged. HOW did you decide what to do about it? Enter this information in your journal.

THINK   ABOUT IT

"Thinking is like loving and dying. Each of us must do it for himself." Josiah Royce

- Draw what you think the inside of your brain looks like when *you* are thinking.

- In your journal, write about **2** things you think about a lot.

- Make up a dictionary entry for: "thinking for yourself."

- In a group, discuss the following: "Too many people don't know what they think until they hear someone else say it."

- Think about _____ ? . Tell someone what it feels like to think

  THiNK!!!

- Spend some time NOT thinking. Discuss with your sharing-partner-for-the-day how easy or difficult it is to "not-think."

- Ask some people (kids and adults) what they think about most often. Publish the results in a news/information sheet.

- Tell your teacher about the most unusual thought you ever had.

The Difference Is

THE DIFFERENCE IS

"How glorious it is, and also how painful it is, to be an exception."

Alfred de Musset

☐ Do something different for a day (write upside-down, walk backwards, wear 2 different shoes . . .) Write 1 sentence about your experience and share it with someone.

☐ With a partner, BRAINSTORM a list of things in our society that "encourage" people to be the SAME (e.g. fashion magazines; the game "Follow the Leader" . . .)

☐ In a group, discuss: •Everybody is different. SO WHAT????
  •You're only as different as you think other people think you are.
  •Why is it hard to accept people, ideas, and things that are different.

☐ Fill in the blank: You know you are different when _____

☐ Close your eyes a moment and create a world in which everybody is EXACTLY the same.
Write a story or a poem about what you "see."

☐ Right now, put your attention on what it would be like to: •be different in appearance
  •have different ideas
  •act differently . . .

In your journal, write about which of these would be hardest for you to accept in other people AND in YOURSELF.

☐ In the circle, tell about a time YOU experienced being different.

☐ Ask some people: "What's normal?" Share the answers with your class.

SUCCESS STORY

SUCCESS STORY

"The toughest thing about success is that you've got to keep on being a success." Irving Berlin

★ Tell someone about a time YOU experienced being successful.

★ Create and design a symbol for success.

★ In your journal, write about which you think is more difficult: "getting to the top" OR "staying there."

★ Interview some people whom you consider to be successful. Ask them what they think you need to know about being successful. Tape the interview or write it like a magazine or newspaper article. Write one or two sentences that tell what you learned from these people.

★ You are successful at _____. Make a poster that advertises your success.

★ In a group, discuss: How do you know when you are a success?
What is success measured by?
What there is BEFORE success/what there is AFTER success . . . .

★ How did you learn about success? Close your eyes and "play-back" the scene. Enter the information in your journal. Tell your sharing-partner-for-the-day and listen to his/her story too.

Me & You

"If you hate a person, you hate something in him that is part of yourself. What isn't part of ourselves doesn't disturb us." **Herman Hesse**

- Close your eyes. Make everything and everyone you hate or have hated disappear from the face of the earth. . . in your journal, write about the changes in your life.

- What is hate? In the circle, tell about a time you experienced hate.

- In a group, discuss:
  What does hating cost you?
  Some people think that extreme hate is a form of love
  How you know when you hate someone/something

- List 5 words that describe ways you act when you hate someone/something.

HATE!

- In your journal, list the qualities that you hate in other people. Next make a list about what you hate in you. When you finish, compare your lists and write 1 sentence about you from this experience.

- Draw a picture of hate.

Remembering

"I can forgive, but I cannot forget," is only another way of saying 'I cannot forgive.'" Henry Ward Beecher

• Create a role play that shows the responsibilities that go along with apologizing to someone / accepting an apology.

   • With another person write 10 different ways to say "I'm sorry." Decide how to practice them.

• Read the poem "This is Just to Say" by William Carlos Williams. Using his format write your own poem apologizing for something you did.

   • Close your eyes: Find your own inner space. Think about something you've done that you wish you hadn't. As fully as possible, re-experience that event and watch it disappear.

• Form a small group to discuss —
   Which is easier: to forgive or apologize?
   How you feel when you apologize.
   Whether it is possible to forget.

   • In your journal, remember —
     10 times you apologized — was it:
     (F) to a friend
     (R) to a relative
     (D) about something you did
     (S) about something you said
     (W) you wished you done sooner

i'm sorry!

   Write 1 or 2 sentences about you from this experience.

GETTING IT

"In this world there are only 2 tragedies. One is not getting what one wants, and the other is getting it." **Oscar Wilde**

● Make a list of what YOU want — write down EVERYTHING that comes to mind. Next to each thing you listed, write possible ways to get it.

● Explain how the dream can sometimes be better than the real thing.

● Write a story with the title: "Too Much of a Good Thing."

● Create a poster or cartoon that shows what you get from this quotation.

● Do a daydream —
  Close your eyes and dream something that is better than what you have. What do you think will happen if you do this everyday? Share your thoughts with a friend.

● With two others, discuss:
  Each moment you live you always get what you want.
  You can only get what you get — nothing else.
  If you don't get anything — what you get is what you get.

  get it?

● In your class, discuss the motto —
  Don't get what you want — want what you get and then you will get what you want.

TIMELESS

"There are two days in the week about which and upon which I never worry . . . One of these days is Yesterday . . . And the other day I do not worry about is Tomorrow."

Robert Jones Burdette

- With two others brainstorm cures for worrying. Try to "sell" your cures to others.

- Interview ten people to try to get a clear description of what it feels like to worry. Summarize your interviews and report to your class.

- Discuss with two others:
  Which is most important to you: your past, your present, your future?
  Why "Today is the first day of the rest of your life."

- Survey the adults in your school on what they worry about. After the survey, chart the results.

- Make a poster that shows HOW TO LIVE FOR TODAY.

- Write an essay on what happens to a problem when you worry about it.

- Make a large poster for your classroom using the words "NOW IS THE ONLY NOW"

THE FINISH LINE

THE FINISH LINE

"Anybody can start something." **James A Shedd**

• Fill in the blanks: I'm proud (glad) I finished _____**?**_____ because _____**?**_____.

• Write a poem about things you wish someone would start and/or finish.

• Close your eyes: you are running a race — see yourself win
                    you are reading a book — read the last page
                    you are baking a cake — take it out of the oven
                    you are fixing a toy — watch it work
                    you are writing a poem — read it to a friend
                    you are _____ — _____

• Describe yourself to someone out of these experiences.

• Make up a dictionary entry for: a quitter.

• Start something (you choose) and finish it. Write yourself a note about which you enjoyed most: starting it, working on it, or finishing it. Which was the hardest for you to do?

• Make a list that tells what you need (or need to do) before you start something.

• Right now, put all your attention on something you started and didn't finish. What would it be like to be something that was started and not finished? Write one sentence that tells what happens to things that are not finished.

• In a group, discuss the following: the value of starting things vs. the value of finishing things.

• In your journal, write how you decide which things to finish in *your* life.

I Gotta Be Me

I GOTTA BE ME . . . .

"Accept me as I am — only then will we discover each other." Federico Fellini

• Take 3 minutes each with another person and ask the questions:

    "Who are you?"
    "When do you pretend?"
    "When are you afraid?"

• What did you find out about yourself?

• Draw a picture of the things (feelings, emotions, experiences, likes/dislikes) that make you, you. This is a non-physical self-portrait.

• Make a map that shows how to discover people. Share your map with your classmates.

• What is acceptance? Write 1 sentence about a time YOU were accepted.

• In your journal, write what you think is the most difficult thing for other people to accept about you.

• Write a poem or story with the title "Changes."

• Write a question and answer about your power to change yourself/other people.

• Draw a picture of "honest."

• Brainstorm with 1 or 2 others: ways to stay true to yourself.

me & you

My World - Welcome!!

"I am a citizen of the world" **Diogenes**

- Discussions for small groups:
  - How you fit into . . . your neighborhood / your city or town / your state / your country / your world / the solar system

  - Why do you think divisions like cities, towns, states, and countries exist?

  - How have TV, film, and satellites made this a world community?

- Activity for the class:
  Brainstorm what it means to be a member of your classroom
  Brainstorm how people get to be accepted members of the class
  Discuss how you can help each other to be a part of the class

- Alone Activity:
  Be by yourself. Close your eyes and see yourself divided among all the places you belong. Sense how it feels to belong. Share this with someone.

- Create a plan (blueprints) for a "world community." (Do this with two others)

hi !

- Write a story about a world in which there are no countries.

- Draw a picture of patriotism and display in your class.

- Look through several newspapers and magazines and cut out articles that concern YOU as a citizen of the world.

the game

MONOPOLY

# of life

THE GAME OF LIFE . . .

"Those who lose today may win tomorrow." **Cervantes**

◆ ◆ ◆ ◆ ◆ ◆

- Close your eyes: see a crystal ball. Look into it and take what you get. Write 1 sentence that tells what you got!

- For 1 day in your class, throw dice to make decisions on problems where there is more than 1 direction you could take. Live by the dice for a day. At the end of the day, have a discussion on: "living by chance." What's the difference?

- Make up a dictionary entry for: "pushing your luck"
  "to luck-out"

- Get some books on astrology and look up your sign. Make a chart for yourself showing which days, months, etc. are best for you. Next time one of these days/months comes up, pay special attention to how you "approach" the day. Out of the experience, write one or two sentences about yourself in your journal.

- Discuss in a group:
  Is it more important to have luck OR skill?
  We're all winners and losers in the game of life
  YOU CAN MAKE IT HAPPEN!

  LUCKY?

- List 5 words that describe the way you act when you feel lucky.

- In your journal, keep a record of *all* the chances you take during one day.

- Write down how you know when to take a chance. After you've "taken it" — then what**???**

- With a partner, agree on some situation and act it out from the point of view of an OPTIMIST. Switch attitudes and roleplay the SAME situation from the point of view of a PESSIMIST.

the head of the class

go to

"To teach is also to learn" **Japanese Proverb**

- Teach anybody anything you know how to do. Describe the experience. What does it take to teach?

- With two others brainstorm things you can't teach anyone. Example: Teach someone to think.

- Teach somebody something you had trouble learning. Try to find a way to make it easier for your student. Write about how you solved the problem or why you weren't able to make it any easier.

- Make a list of things you need to know before you teach.

- In a small group teach someone to: talk
  walk
  stand
  listen

  ⇨ **teacher**

  learner ⬅

- Class activity:
  Decide to spend one whole day in your class learning from each other. The class (pupils and teachers) are all teachers. Your job is to be prepared to "teach" something, (that might mean share, show, talk, listen, walk with, be with etc.) to some of your classmates and teacher. Record what you do to prepare for this. (If you can, have a TV recorder available to record your day.)

- In your journal, write about the most important thing you've ever learned.

FREE PLAY

FREE PLAY

"Half our life is spent trying to find something to do with the time we have rushed thru life trying to save." **Will Rogers**

• Do nothing for 10 minutes — so what??? Tell someone "what."

• Make a collage of things that "give" people more free time (examples: TV dinners, pampers, xerox machines, typewriters, etc.)

• List 5 words that describe the feeling of time.

• Ask some people this question: "What do you do when you have nothing to do?" Publish the results.

• Make up a dictionary entry for: "leisure shock."

• Discuss in a group:

    Is time "free?"
    Is it possible to make up for lost time?
    More time often becomes too much time
    Can time be saved?

6:22   4:58   7:15   12:03   9:00

• Close your eyes and ask yourself what it feels like to "kill" time. Write one or two sentences about your experience of this.

• Close your eyes and run the "movie" of your classroom in sloooow motion. What happens? Tell your sharing-partner-for-the-day.

GIVE and TAKE

"Happy are those who can give without remembering and take with forgetting."

• Class discussions:
   The difference between giving THINGS away and giving of YOURSELF
   It is better to give than to receive
   It is better to receive than to give
   How you decide what to give someone

• Make a collage of things you would like to be able to give to other people.

• Write a fable called "The First Gift Ever."

• Next time you receive something don't say THANK YOU — instead say, I feel (felt) ———————— when you gave me ————.

THANKS...

• In your journal, write:
   All the things you'd like your friends to give you.
   All the things you could give to your friends.

• With two others, brainstorm:
   All the things you could say or do when you receive something from someone.

• Write a thank you note to someone and thank that person for something s/he has done for you . . . . . SEND IT.

BELIEVE IT

of NOT

"Nil credam et omnia cavebo." (Believe nothing and be on guard against everything). Latin Prov

- Take a "Trust Walk." Choose a partner and have that person take you for a walk around school. (YOU wear a blindfold). After, discuss with your partner:

  your experience   if your partner was able to take care of you

  if trust developed   how you felt/how your partner felt

  Switch roles and do it again.

- Make up a dictionary entry for: "losing faith."

- Discuss in a group: People believe what they want to believe

  "I have to make it all by myself in this world"

  How you know when to believe someone

- Draw the difference between UNbelievable and NOT believable.

- Write 1 sentence that tells how you think your instincts work.

- Make some warning signs to show people things they should beware of.

- Close your eyes: you are setting your alarm clock

  you ask someone in the street for directions

  you bake cookies using a recipe in a magazine

  you take the medicine your doctor prescribes for you

  you buy something and the clerk hands you your change

  your friend tells you that a movie you want to see is terrible . . .

  . . .place a mark on a scale of 1 - 10 that shows your trust level for each one . . .

  <u>don't trust at all</u>   <u>trust completely</u>

  1 _____ 10

- Fill in the blanks: My instincts were correct when _____ .

  I was fooled the time I   _____ .

- Next time you find yourself trusting (someone, yourself, something), pay special attention to the "risks" you are taking. Write a note to yourself about these risks.

incredible

- Make some warning signs to show people things they should be beware of.

- Describe yourself to someone out of this experience.

CHANGES

"There is nothing permanent except change." **Heraclitus**

• Keep a "Change Diary" for one month — noting any changes in yourself, the environment, other people, things, the world . . . . Write about these changes (and/or illustrate them): HOW, WHEN, WHAT, WHY, ETC.

• Do a collage on — How I've changed in the last week . . . in the last year . . . in the last 5 years . .

• Go outside or look out a window. Find something to watch that you know will be there for some time. Look carefully and describe the thing you have chosen to observe. Pay attention to details. One hour later, look again and note any changes. Do the same one hour after that, two hours later, and the next day. Discuss the question: did what you were watching change OR did you change your watching style?

• Alone activity: Close your eyes — find some space — Imagine you are only the reflection of someone identical to you, just below the surface of where you are standing or sitting. When he or she walks, you walk. When he or she raises a hand — you do. What does this have to do with change or permanance?

• Class meeting topics:
  Nothing changes — we only change how we see things.
  Change is usually violent not peaceful.

• With several others, discuss three major changes that have taken place in your lifetime.

• Make a time-line that shows how people change as they get older. Share your finished time-line with your class.

the "IN" crowd

"One man with courage makes a majority." Andrew Jackson

• Make up a dictionary entry for: a majority of one.

gulp!

• Tell your sharing-partner-for-the-day about a time you experienced courage.

• Right now put all of your attention on being all alone on something. Notice everything about it. What would it be like to go against the majority? Can you let yourself "feel" it for a few seconds? Now, write a single sentence that satisfies you about your experience. Give it to your teacher.

• In your journal, write about how courage is "physical" and/or "mental." How do you know?

• Discuss in a group:

> The advantages/disadvantages of "following the crowd."
> Many people believe that the majority rules — who rules in the following situations? In your family/ school/ in the U.S./ among the friends you have/ in organized sports/ in your community?
> Is it a majority and why do you think things are this way?

• Trace a Peanuts cartoon but leave the word balloons blank. Fill in the dialogue yourself . . .
TOPIC: peer pressure.

• At different times in life people find themselves in and out of many majority and minority groups — for example, if you are a student going to school, you are part of a majority group (there are more students than teachers in schools). At the same time you might be part of a minority group in a different way — for example, if you are a twin or a Native American, or you are left-handed, you are in the minority in this country. (However, if almost everyone in your family is left-handed, then you are part of the majority in your family.) Make a list of the majority and minority groups you belong to. After completing your list, write 2 sentences about yourself.

HIDE AND SEEK

"A man went looking for America. And couldn't find it anywhere." **(ad for "Easy Rider")**

★Make an outline of the United States (large) — fill the inside with words that you think tell what this country is.

★Close your eyes — find your space: re-visit America. Take some time to go places you've been or want to be at. Describe your trip to your sharing-partner-for-the-day.

★Take a tour of America via the library. Stop in any three states you would like to visit and do some research on what's there — what they produce, major cities, interesting facts, tourist attractions, population, sports teams, etc. Make GIANT—SIZE picture postcards to present your information to the class. On one side, make some kind of picture about the state and on the other side, (in postcard letter-writing style!) present your facts.

★Interview some people about what America needs today. Publish the results in a class information sheet or newsletter.

★In a group, discuss:

How it is possible to "lose" a country
See America first . . . WHY?
What is the "American Dream?"

★Write a poem about your piece of America.

★List 5 words that describe the way you feel about America.

★Find one or two other people — compose, rehearse, and present to the class a skit with the title: "Scenes from America."

★With a partner, make a "balance-sheet" for America — read (or listen) to the words of some patriotic songs (like: "America the Beautiful" and "The Star Spangled Banner") and/or American documents (like: The Gettysburg Address and The Declaration of Independence). On one side of your sheet, list what America is *supposed* to be, and on the other side, list what America *is*.

talking to YOURSELF

> *"Conscience is the inner voice which warns us that someone may be looking."* H. L. Mencken

- Draw a picture of your conscience.

- Trace a cartoon, and leave the word balloons blank. Fill in the dialogue yourself. *Topic*: The hardest thing about having a conscience.

- In your journal, list 3 people who you wouldn't want looking when you make a mistake. Explain your choices.

- In a group, discuss: How does a person "get" a conscience?
  What your conscience does/doesn't do for you
  It doesn't matter who is looking! Why?

- Write a poem with the title: "Livin' With My Conscience."

- Write one or two sentences that tells how YOUR conscience works.

- Close your eyes . . ."see" yourself when . . .
    - you haven't studied for an important test
    - someone you don't like wants to borrow a pencil
    - a sales clerk at a store gives you too much change
    - you break something you've borrowed from a friend
    - you want to go to the movies but you don't have enough money to pay full price —
      you look young
    - you return something to a store that you don't want

 . . . in your journal, list as *many* alternatives that come into your mind for what you MIGHT (could) do, and then, write what your "consience tells you to do."

- Write yourself a reminder about a time you didn't listen to your conscience — what happened?

- In your journal, write about: how *you* decided what is right and what is wrong.

SURPRISE!

"The only completely consistent people are the dead." **Aldous Huxley**

- Journal work:

    Think of a situation in which you always act the same way. List the things you gain and lose by acting the same way all the time. Plan how you could change your behavior to make the situation better. Next time it comes up, try it out.

- List 20 habits that you have. After each of them, place one of the following depending on how you feel about your habit:

    -- very negative
    - negative
    0 neutral
    + positive
    + + very positive

Collect the negative ones and see if you can identify a pattern for yourself. What could you do about the negaive habits in your life? How much of it has to do with changing how you look at yourself?

- Be a *new* YOU for a day. First, change as much about your physical appearance as possible (e.g. if you usually wear jeans to school, dress-up, or change your hairstyle). Find a new way to come to school (walk down different streets or go by yourself/or with different people). Try to make other changes in your "patterns." Eat something new for lunch; if you always wear a watch, leave it home; write with a colored felt tip pen instead of a ballpoint; if you're always early, be on time; ETC.

Write about the experience, how you felt, other people's reactions, what you learned, and what things you would/wouldn't try again. Share your experiment with your class or a small group.

- Write a poem about some of the patterns in your life, OR what you think the patterns in you life will be 10 years from now.

- What would you do if:

    you got to school and everyone was walking backwards
    your family announced you would be eating breakfast for dinner and dinner for breakfast
    you turned on the TV and all the programs were being broadcast in a strange language
    the weather report said there was a blizzard going on outside and all you can see is bright sunshine

- As a class, discuss what CONSISTENCY gets for you/ protects you from/ costs you.

HOORAY FOR ME!

"You're greater than you think you are."

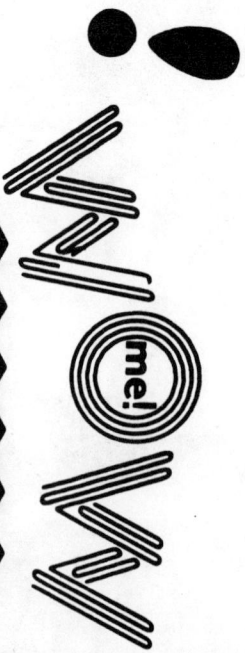

WOW me!

★ Sing your praises. In your journal, make a list of everything that's terrific about YOU.

★ Write an autobiographical poem about the great things you've done. Share it with someone.

★ Fill in the blanks: I really like myself when _____
The greatest thing I've ever done _____
I shouldn't be so down on myself about _____
_____

★ Write down ways you tell yourself you're okay . . . and how you let other people know. Let someone else know!

★ "How I celebrate myself" . . . design a billboard to share with the world.

★ Have an "I'm Great At That" trade-off. On an index card, write a "classified ad" for yourself describing something you do really well (ANYTHING from baking delicious brownies to being the best pass receiver to having the neatest-looking handwriting.) Post in a special place (like a bulletin board — check with your teahcer) and answer at least one ad for something you'd like to know how to do. Be prepared in case somebody answers yours!

★ Discuss in a group: Where people get their ideas about what they are.
"I'm perfect the way I am."

COME INTO MY

LABORATORY

★ ★

"Discovery consists on seeing what everybody else has seen and thinking what nobody else has thought."
★ ★ ★ ★ ★ ★ ★ ★ ★ ★ ★ ★ ★

• The best thing I ever discovered . . . close your eyes and re-create the scene. What was the experience like? Enter this information in your journal.

• Invent new uses for:

ping pong balls   can opener   shoelaces   umbrella   money   scotch tape   ice cream   gloves

❋choose **3** — make a chart that shows your ideas.

• In your journal, write about: How you get your ideas and how you decide if your ideas are any good.

• Often people say, "Gee, there really should be a better way to . . . .," or, "If only there were . . . .," or, "Someone really ought to invent . . . ." Around a circle, (with at least 5 or 6 other people), name some of the problems and brainstorm ways to solve them.

AHA!

• Discuss in a group: Whether or not EVERYTHING has been done
         What "new" frontiers are there left to explore?
         The importance of doing something that has never been done before

• Brainstorm with a partner: How to get rid of pollution
                   How to weigh an elephant
                   How to make a fire-proof building
                   How to make hair so you don't have to comb it
                   How to make shoes so you can walk on water

?

• Close your eyes and "see" yourself alongside a famous inventor. (If you need to, do research to find out who invented what you think is a great or interesting invention). See yourself in that time and place, helping to share in the discovery. Write a story about the experience, called ___(name of inventor)___ and ME.

• Try this experiment with a partner: You both need a stack of unlined paper and crayons (colors should be the same for both of you). Copy this list of "things" for your partner — a box / a ball / an apple / a house / a child / water / joy. Sit so that you cannot see what the other is doing. Draw the things on the list. (Work any way you want — large, small, many colors, one color . . . . try not to let what you think your partner will do influence you). When you both are finished, compare the drawings, Write 1 or 2 sentences in you journal about the way people "SEE" things from this experience.

SMILE

"It is not how much we have, but how much we enjoy, that makes happiness."

◆ ◆ ◆

• Finish this story: "Once upon a time . . . in the Land of Everything, the birds sang sweetly, the trees touched the bright, blue sky, the flowers bloomed all year long and the sun always shone. It was a land where the football players never got injured, where the baseball players only hit homeruns, and everyone had enough food, money, and peanut butter. Everyone was happy. Everything was perfect . . . . OR WAS IT

• Do something you enjoy. What about it gives you pleasure? Make a journal entry.

• With several of your classmates design a bumper-sticker about happiness. Sell them after you make them.

• Make a happiness book. Brainstorm what happiness is and fill your book with drawings, song, stories, poems, colors, words, etc., that illustrate your list.

• In a small group, discuss: Happiness is one of those things you can't run after.
  Whether happiness is self-created or other-created.
  The kinds of things you find in people you enjoy.
  Where you find happiness.

hAppY iS . . .

Alone activity:
  Close your eyes and enjoy something that makes you happy. Spend time each day enjoying something with your eyes closed. In your journal, write about the difference between doing "it" and doing it "in your mind."

HOME SWEET HOME

"Home is not where you live, but where they understand you."

Brainstorm with another person a list of all the things a "home" is.

• Design your ideal room. Do NOT put any furniture it in. Instead, fill your room with people and ideas that will make it a place where you are understood.

• Fill in the blanks: A place where I would like to live is ___?___ because ___?___.

• Close your eyes — find your space: see your home from a distance. Be away for a month and see yourself come home. Experience what happens when you walk in. Tell your sharing-partner-for-a-day. Listen to his/her story too.

• Write 1 sentence that describes how you feel when people don't understand you.

• What do people need to understand about YOU? Make a list and show it to your teacher and four other people.

• Write some suggestions for making your home a more comfortable place . . . take these home and discuss with your family.

• Make a chart that shows "HOW TO UNDERSTAND PEOPLE."

• Where I'm Understood . . . enter this information in your journal.

My Home...

❀ Be careful not to...

1 pound small new potatoes
1½ to 2 pounds fresh peas
   Lightly salted boiling water
½ cup light cream

½ teaspoon Salad ...
½ teaspoon salt, or to taste
1 tablespoon butter
⅛ teaspoon Cracked Black Pep...

Scrape new potatoes; shell peas. Cook potatoes and peas separately
lightly salted boiling water. Drain and combine potatoes and pea...
cream just to simmering; crush Salad Herbs and add to cream alo...
salt and butter. Pour over peas and potatoes; let stand for 3 or 4...
Taste and add additional salt if desired. Mix again carefully. Spri...
Pepper and serve at once. Makes 6 servings.

Sweet Potatoes with Orange and Ginger

1 can (1 lb. 7 oz.) syrup-pack sweet
   potatoes
¼ cup honey
2 teaspoons Orange Peel

1 teaspoon finely chop...
   lized Ginger
1 tablespoon butter

Drain and reserve liquid from sweet potatoes. Arrange sweet
baking dish. Combine liquid with honey, Orange Peel, and c...
Pour over sweet potatoes. Dot with butter. Bake in a 375° o...
minutes or until sweet potatoes are well glazed. Serve hot. M...

Baked Onions

4 very large dry yellow onions
1 cup hot water
2 teaspoons Chicken Seasoned Stock
   Base
1 tablespoon butter
1 teaspoon salt

2 teaspoons hone...
¼ teaspoon Leme...
¼ teaspoon Papr...
.2 tablespoons b...
   or finely ch...

...in half and arrange in large casserole
...ter. salt, honey, Lem...

---

an accompaniment
...onds as a variation.

...utter
...rrowroot
...water chestnuts
...i Yen Seasoning
...ne Grind Black Pepper

...se until tender. Drain;
... 1 cup) to make 1½
...eat and stir in Arrow-
...tly, until thickened and
...cream sauce along with
...at thoroughly and serve

...favorite especially flavorful.

...poon Mei Yen Seasoning
...poon Spice Parisienne
...s (8 oz. each) tomato sauce
...p hot water
...p dry white wine
...p shredded sharp Cheddar
...cheese

...ds and stems; wash pep-
...Hot stand

"Tell me what you eat and I will tell you who you are" Savarin

•With several of your classmates make lists of everything you ate yesterday and today. By looking at your list try to describe who you are.

•Write a poem about a food that loves you. Share it with the class.

•Journal Activity: Brainstorm way that food influences you.

YUM...

•Get together with three or four others and plan a role play to include the following:

A food that is —

mysterious   careless   sincere   angry   smart

evil,   sensitive   amusing   friendly   attractive

Pick 4 of the above and choose your way to show these "food personalities."

•Go to the library and borrow a cookbook. Read through it and find a recipe that sounds like you. Copy it and see if anyone can guess why you choose it.

•Get your class to watch some TV commercials that advertise food. What is America, based on its food advertisements?

•Class project:
Imagine that a Martian has landed and has just knocked on your door. It's up to you to serve the Martian a "typical" American meal. What will you serve and why? Design a menu for the meal you serve so the Martian can take it home as a souvenir.

•Alone activity:
Close your eyes and get comfortable. Imagine your breakfast going into your mouth and body. Watch the trip it takes in you body. Share your experience with a friend.

•Class discussion:
It has just been found out that JELLO has brainwaves!!!

M-O-R-E

OR LESS

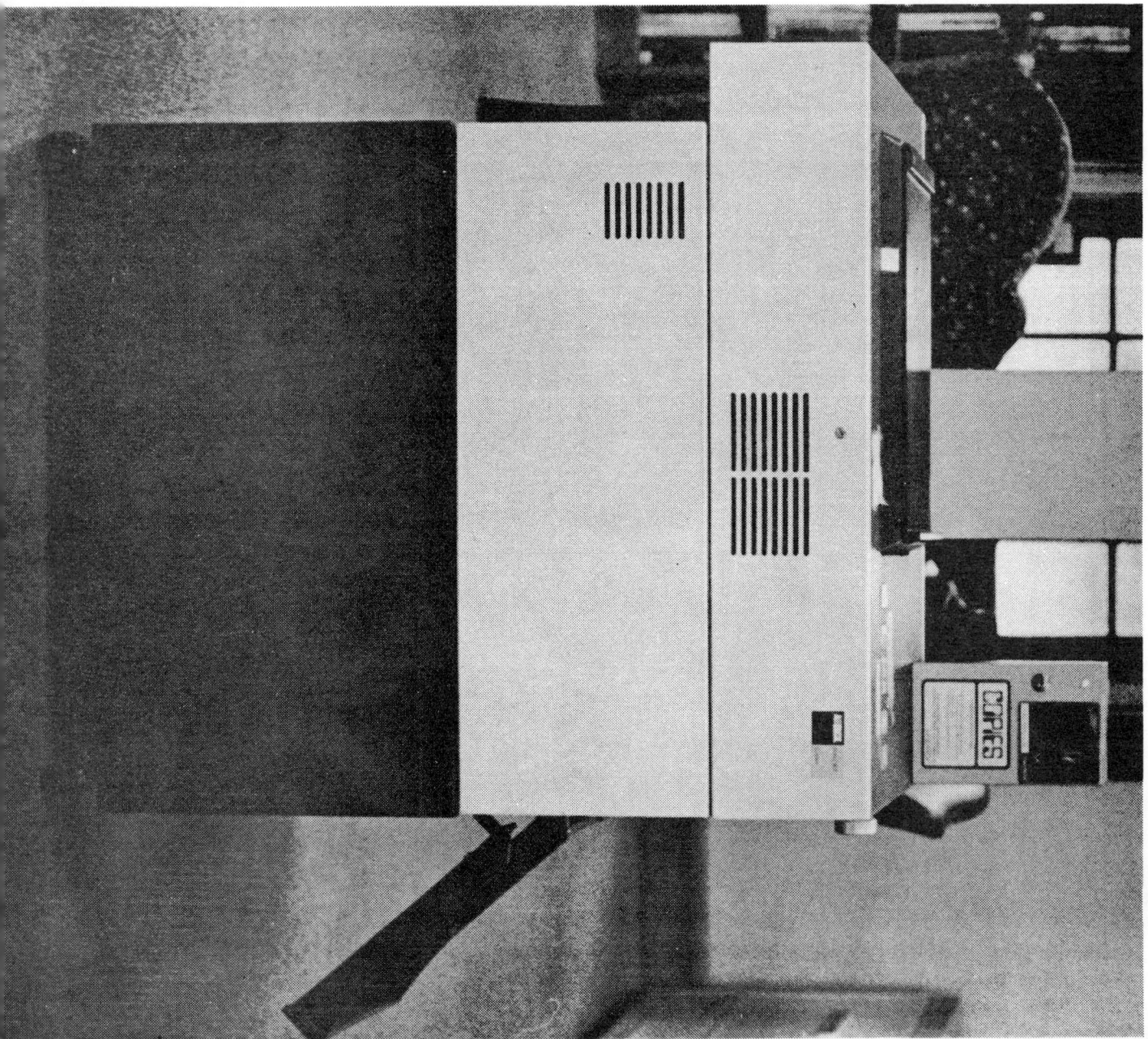

❀❀ "A single rose can be my garden." ❀❀

UNIQUE *

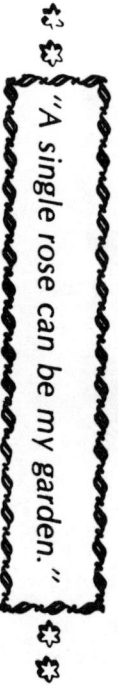

✱ Make a collage (or find another way to show) those things that are SPECIAL in your life.

✱ Class discussions:
If more is always better or if less is always worse.
How advertising makes people feel that they want a whole garden instead of a rose.
How paying attention to something can make it more important.
How you know when you've had enough.

✱ Write about something you have that is special because it is scarce.

✱ Journal activity: Imagine that you can choose only one thing (that you own now) to keep forever. Explain your choice.

✱ With 2 others:
Bring some flowers to school. Spend at least five minutes looking very carefully at your garden. Share what new things you notice. Find something else to notice. Try not to evaluate what you see. Just notice.

A GRAND OPENING

★★★★★★
A GRAND OPENING
★★★★★★
★★★★★
★★★★★
★★★★★

"Open your mind and say 'Ah'"

☆ As a class brainstorm ways to open your mind. Design some ways for this to happen in your class.

☆ Illustrate the difference between a closed mind & an open mind.

☆ Discuss with a friend: You have the chance to rent a mind for a day. Whose mind would you rent and why?

☆ Do some whips with the class:
Something I've learned that suprised me . . . . .
My mind is . . . .
Whatever comes to mind . . . .
Something that is mind-boggling. . . .

☆ Write a recipe for: BRAIN-FOOD. After, trade recipes with someone else.

☆ Write some questions you would like to have answered about the human mind. Share your questions in a small group and brainstorm possible answers.

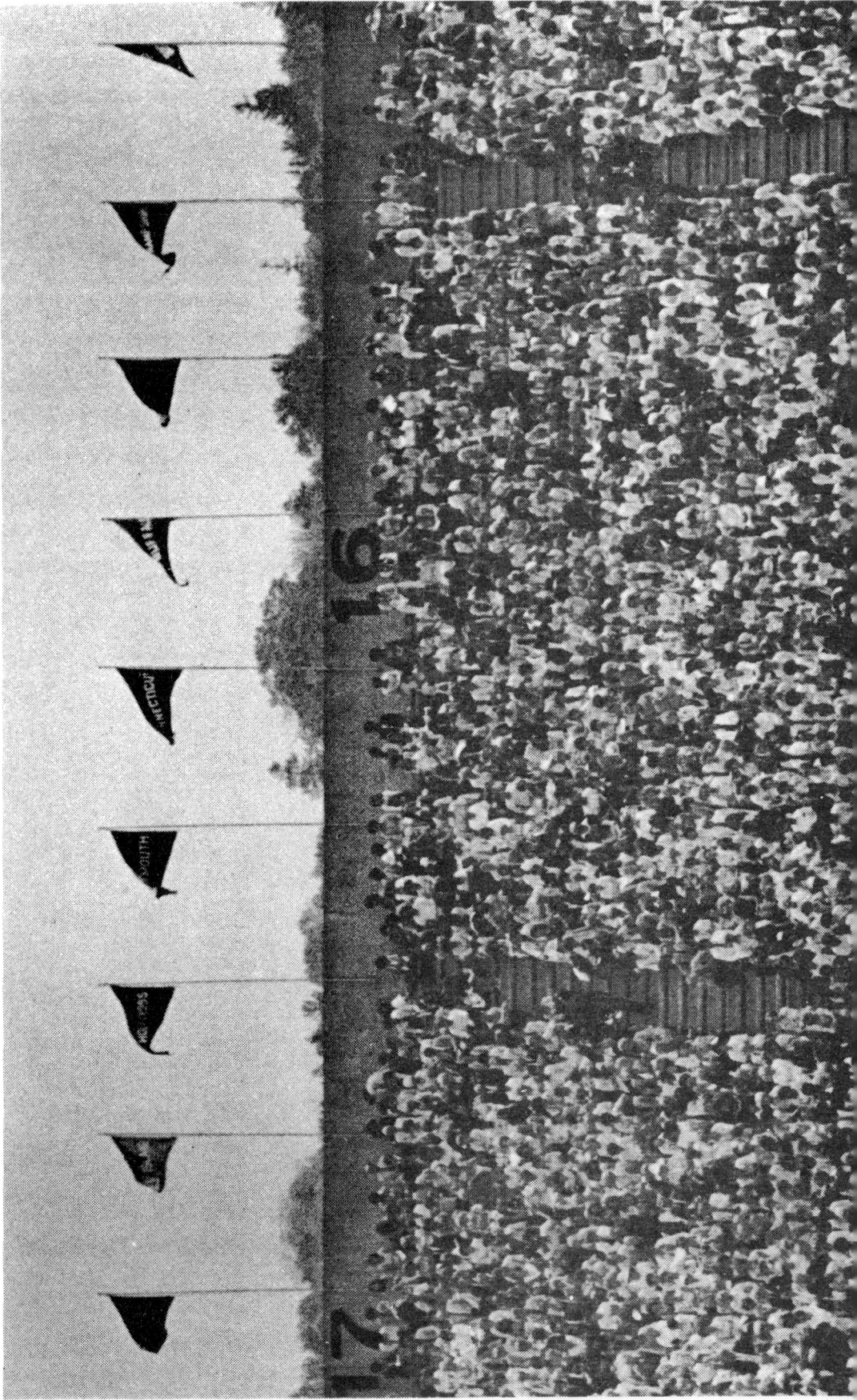

people are strange

PEOPLE ARE STRANGE

"A stranger is a friend you haven't met."

strange!

● Write a recipe for: How to meet people.

● Draw what you think your 1st impression looks like.

● Write 10 different ways to say hello. Practice them.

● Close your eyes and create a scene with you as the new kid in school. What would it be like? Can you let yourself pretend to be "it" for a few seconds? Now, write a sentence about your experience. Share it with someone.

● How do you treat people you don't know? With 1 or 2 other people, "try-out" some 1st meetings (encounters) . . . consider: body language, facial expression, attitude. Talk about the messages being sent.

● Discuss in a group: *How you can feel lonely in a crowded room

　　　　*The importance/unimportance of first impressions

　　　　*How you decide whether or not you want to meet someone

● In your journal, write down your ideas about how a stranger can turn into a friend and how a friend can turn into a stranger.

YOU'RE NÖT

ALONE

"Rain does not fall on one roof alone" **Cameroonian Proverb**

- With three others design a game which demonstrates how people are similar.

- In your journal, describe the feelings of togetherness you feel in your classroom, family and community.

- With another person brainstorm a list of "experiences" that most people have in common. Put them into categories and share them with your class.

- Write a poem or song called "We're All in This Together."

- Write another proverb with the same message.

- Close your eyes and get comfortable — pick out a person in your class. Look into a mirror and the reflection you'll see will be that person. Do the following:

  - Change clothes with them
  - Smile and they will frown
  - Frown and they will smile
  - Have them looking in the mirror at you
  - Exchange hairdos
  - Raise your arm and see what they do
  - Return their clothes
  - Return their hair
  - Have them have your face with their clothes
  * Who is who?

ALL OF US!!!

- With a small group discuss:
  - If another person can experience your experiences
  - Misery loves company

THE *WORD* IS...

"Every definition is dangerous." **Erasmus**

● In your journal, write your OWN definitions for the following words: (be as specific as you can) beautiful/ / funny / tall / dog / America / family. Compare your definitions to the dictionary's. How are they alike/different? Which are better ? Why?

Words etc.

● Write a poem that has no words.

● Design a collage of your favorite words.

● In a small group, discuss:
  • A time no words were right
  • How you know what words mean
  • Can words mean anything you want them to mean?
  • Words do not mean anything themselves — the only meanings they have are the meanings that people give to them

● Do a project: find out how new words are added to the language and how people learn what they mean. Share the results of your research with your class.

● As a classroom experiment, place a well-known object (feather, pencil, stone, etc.) in front of your class. Ask them to write a definition of this item. Take the time to read the definitions aloud to see how they are alike or different. Spend some time discussing the reasons people see things differently.

REMEMBER WHAT?

> *"We do not remember days, we remember moments."* **Cesare Pavese**

~ Make a chart that shows: How to Remember Something. Post in your class for others to read.

~ Close your eyes and pretend that you can have someone else's memories for a day . . . whose memories do you want and why? In your journal, write about some of the memories you expect to have.

~ Write a poem about some of your best memories and share it with someone.

~ Close your eyes and re-create someone or something from your past. Try to focus in on the feeling of "having" a memory instead of the memory itself. Write one sentence that tells where you feel your memories.

~ Fill in the blanks: A memory is _____
　　　　　　　　　Memories are great for _____ .

~ Respond to the phrase: "STOP, a moment." Tell someone what you get.

HuH?

~ In a group, discuss: No day is over if you have the memory of it
　　　　　　　　　　Why you remember some things and forget other things

~ Choose **3** of these memories and tell your sharing-partner-for-the-day.
Listen to his/her stories too.

- a PLACE I remember . . .
- a SOUND I remember . . .
- a TASTE I remember . . .
- a SMELL I remember . . .
- a TEXTURE I remember . . .
- a FEELING I remember . . .
- a PERSON I remember . . .

a leave of ABSENCE

"To leave is to die a little . . . One leaves behind a little of oneself/ At any hour, any place." **Edmond Haraucourt**

● Imagine that today you are leaving your school and neighborhood forever. Share with someone what people will remember about you (what you will leave behind).

● With two others, brainstorm a list of ways to say "GOODBYE." Practice them.

● In a small group, discribe how it feels to have to say goodbye.

● Conduct a circletime on this topic: The worst thing about leaving . . . . . .

● Write a letter to someone you haven't seen in a long time. Mail it!

● With another person, brainstorm ways to "keep in touch" with people, places, and things.

● As a class project: listen to the radio for songs about people leaving one another. Analyze what they say about goodbyes and loneliness. Discuss whether or not these songs are realistic.

● Write a poem about the things people have left behind for YOU.

● With a small group, discuss whether or not the memories of people and the things they leave behind can substitute for the "real thing."

● Close your eyes: Experience people in your mind. Who comes to visit you? Listen to your conversation. Comment in your journal about your visit.

IT COULD be BetteR

..., Pols And Press Blast ...ario Fo's Italian TV Program

By FRANK WERBA

Rome, April 26.

...cation pervading the ...iusting Corp. (RAI) ...st four Sunday night Franco Zeffirelli's ...zareth" ended and a ...roversy enveloped the ...days before the final ...ent on the tube.

...a violent attack from ...ad from Rome's lead- Cardinal Poletti, was ...RAI-TV for its spon- ...atirc. "blasphemous" ...ed, directed and per- ...rio Fo.

...his reappearance for ...absence of 14 years, ...riod he has headed a ...theatre group and has ...eries of original shows ...plays) marked by ...conformism and re- ...rades against all poli- ...to the right of his own ...ving views that made ...of all political parties ...mmunists to the far ...fill Thursday night ...ot by Channel II's top ...Fichera. Fo was given ...gs for a show. General- ...c Devil's Herald" (or ...ter"). Debut seg. 90 ...ned on page 78.

First 3 Segs Of 'Roots' Good Draw On BBC-TV

London, April 26.

"Roots," the Warner Bros.-David Wolper miniseries grinding here via BBC-TV in six 90-minute seg- ments, pulled very respectable numbers on the basis of ratings thus far for the first three segs.

The three aired on consecutive nights over the Easter holiday weekend, with the first two making the top 20 golden circle for the week via the Jicar meter sampling. Both clocked more than 6,500,000 total

(Continued on page 85)

See Radio Gross Over $3-Bil In '85

Washington, April 26.

With sales spurred by quadro- phonics and AM stereo, the Na- tional Assn. of Broadcasters pre- dicts the U.S. will be stocked with 560,000,000 radios in 1985, about 2.4 per person. It says revenues for the radio industry will see a similar in- crease by that year — as much as an 85% jump to $3.2-billion.

The rosy outlook is included in "Radio in 1985," a six-month study conducted for the NAB by Frazier, Gross. and Clay, a broadcast con-

(Continued on page 86)

DAVE KINGMAN

I loved RINGLING BROS. AND BARNUM & BAILEY CIRCUS as a child and still do as an adult. It's pure enjoyment. It has the same thrilling element as a sporting event — you don't know what's going to happen next. The wonderment fasci- nates me.

New York Mets.

Bad Odor From Cuffo Tix For Conn. Jai Alai

Hartford, April 26.

A Stamford financier was the man who recently brought the state gaming commission to heel. Forced to resign his post as head of the Bridgeport Jai Alai fronton by the State gaming commission, Hyman

National Endowment Sings Up In High G's

Washington, April 26.

The National Endowment for the Arts has a new way of pitching for films and more coin from a tightfisted Congress. It sings for its subsidy.

During otherwise stodgy hear- ings last week before the Senate Ap- propriations Subcommittee, Metropolitan Opera chirp Carmen Balthrop sparked her testimony with an aria from Puccini's "Turan- dot."

NEA is asking Capitol Hill to fund a 1978 budget of $123,700,000.

Mel Brooks Creates The Whole Thing

Hollywood, April 26.

For his new pic, "High Anxiety," which rolled Monday (25) in San Francisco for 20th-Fox, Mel Brooks is billed not only as star and direc- tor but also as producer, cowriter, and title song composer-lyricist.

It's possible that Brooks is the first man in film history to wear all these hats on a single major pic—a claim which is hard to verify, parti- cularly since Charlie Chaplin rou- tinely was star, producer, director, writer, and musical composer-con- ductor of his films

And Josef Von Sternberg, on his last film, "The Saga Of Anatahan," was director, producer, writer, nar-

Friars Toast Kirk Douglas With More Raves Tha

By JOE C...

The Friars lit ... Douglas as its an... year at its annual ... American Hotel,... (23), shifted the se... soiree from a reas... continues in swell... gathered about 1,... and $150 to attend...

The soiree was ... man of distinction ... Friars insomuch ... and featured a dai... single comedian ... honor for the first ...

However, it was... There are certain ... cannot be kept in... leavening hand of... particularly Geor... Howard Cosell di... of the occasion. E... moments, shared ... of the time that ... wouldn't let the... closeup of Kirk's... As several spea... sion remarked, t... were used up for... they did was to ... acter of the ev...

(Continued ...)

...SE IN JAZZ ...TE WITH CUBA

...w Orleans, April 25. ...ned on page 78.

Sherpa Guides Save

"People ask you for criticism, but they only want praise." **W. Somerset Maugham**

the critic in YOU...

- Find **10** *less* painful ways to say, "That's awful." Practice saying them.

- Fill in the blanks: Some criticism that hurt _____ .
    I've learned from criticism that _____ .
    Criticism is good for _____ .
    Being criticized is difficult because _____ .

- In a group, discuss: "We all need to be loved"
    YOU are the only person you have to please
    People are their own worst critics
    It's easy to be a critic

- Write down something you say to yourself when you are criticized.

- With a partner, BRAINSTORM: How To Be A Good Critic.

- With a group of 4 or 5 people, PLAY "Rate the Record" or "TV Show," or "Fast Food Restaurant" or **?** . Before you begin, make a list of 6-10 items you want to rate, and another list of *general* things you expect from a record or **?** . Every person in the group writes a 1-2 sentence "critical review" for each item on the list. When all are finished, "compare notes." Use the list of expectations as a guide.

!!!#!##!!!!#!!

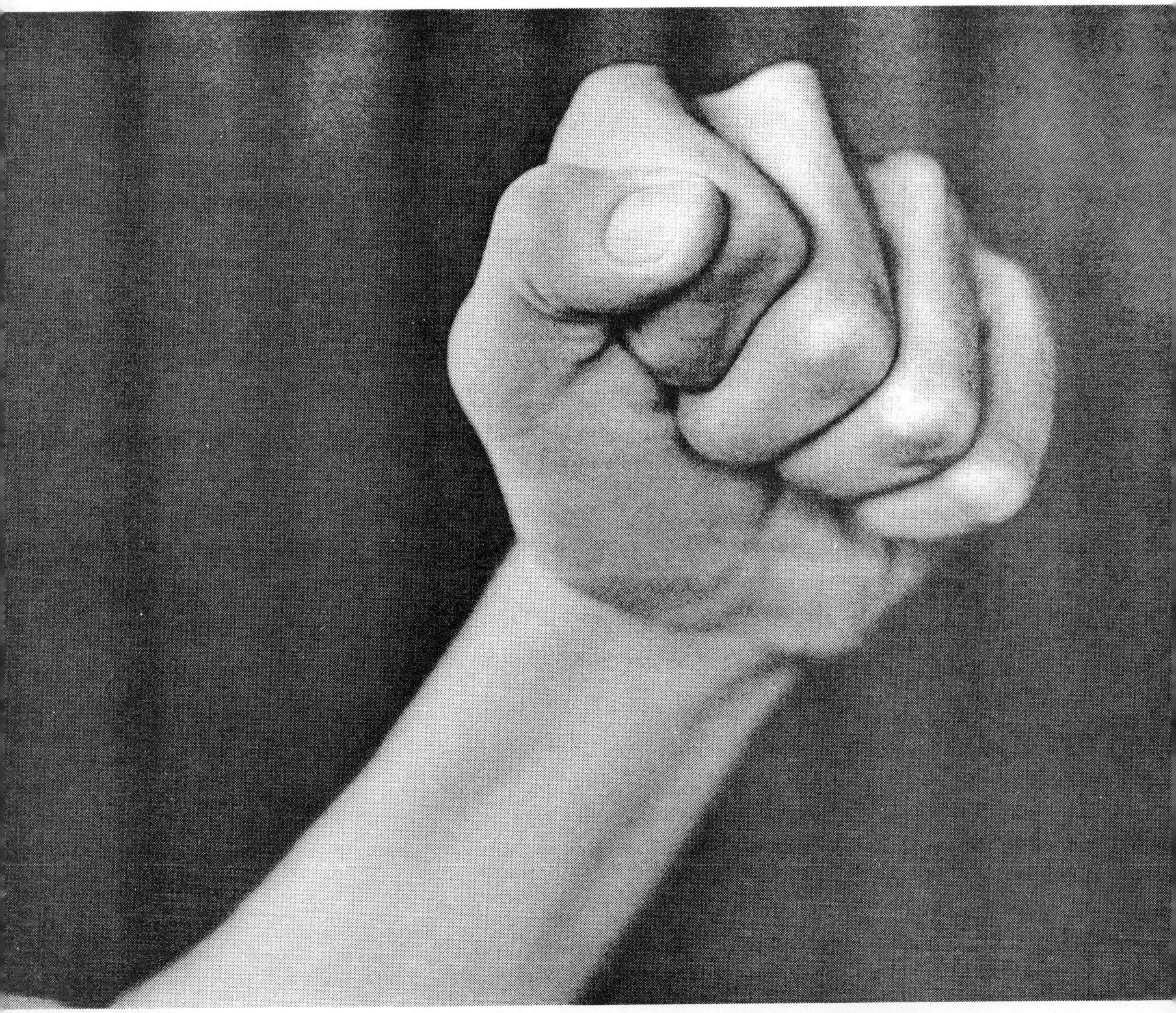

!!!##@#!@@###!!

"Anybody can become angry — that is easy; but to be angry with the right person, and to the right degree, and at the right time, and for the right purpose, and in the right way — that is not within everybody's power and is not easy." **Aristotle**

• With another person, BRAINSTORM a list of what people can do with their anger.

• In your journal, write: Things my anger gets for me . . . . costs me . . . .

• Find 1 or 2 people, compose, rehearse and present to the class a skit entitled: DON'T BUG ME!

• List 5 words that describe the things you do whenever you are angry.

• With a partner, discuss: How you can tell when a person is getting angry
                            YOU are the only person responsible for your anger

• Write a note to someone about things that make you angry.

GRR...

• Fill in the blanks: Anger is the color of _____.
                     Anger sounds like _____.
                     Anger touches me _____.

• Close your eyes. Focus in on a time that you were very angry. Wait a few seconds and "feel" your anger dissolving. How do you stop feeling angry? Where does your anger go? What do you feel in its place? Enter this information in your journal. Share your experience with someone.

• Practice "letting go" of your anger.

RRRED

turning

"Man is the only animal that blushes. Or needs to." Mark Twain

rrrred....

• With a small group, discuss: Your ability to laugh at yourself
Where do you feel your embarrassment
How you handle your embarrassment
Describe how it feels to be embarrassed
Is embarrassment self-created or other-created

• With one of your classmates, interview some people in your school on the topic of "embarrassment." Ask questions like:

   1. Describe some times when you are embarrassed

   2. What do you think causes embarrassment?

   3. What are some things you say to yourself when you blush?

• Summarize the results and share with the class.

• In your journal, write about things that make you self-conscious.

• Write a fable that explains why people are the *only* animals who blush.

• Brainstorm a list of what's happening when people get embarrassed.

• Do a circletime on this topic: A time I was really embarrassed . . . .

• With several of your classmates brainstorm: what you can do when you start to blush.

IT COULD **BE**

IT COULD BE

"So many worlds, so much to do/ So little done, such things to be." **Alfred Lord Tennyson**

❏Draw the difference between "possible" and "actual."

PERHAPS

❏Write at least *3* potential endings to these situations:
    2 cars are coming directly at each other at 50mph or a super highway
    a person has left his/her wallet on the bus
    a football team is losing by 1 point with seconds left in the game and they have the ball

❏What is the potential of: a piece of wood . . . ?   a dream . . . ?
                          a $10 bill . . . ?   a match . . . ?
                          a smile . . . ?   a piece of paper . . . ?
                          a lie . . . ?   a compliment . . . ?
❏Discuss the possibilities with your sharing-partner-for-the-day.

❏Write a poem about WHAT COULD BE.

MAYBE

❏Write 1 sentence that tells about *your* potential as a person.

❏In a group, discuss: What makes things happen the way they do?
                       How do you know when you're "living up to your potential?"
                       Where does your potential come from?

❏In your journal, tell why you are *free* to be anyone and anything.

WHY NOT?

Once upon a time

"Dragons are too seldom." (Puppeteers in South Dakota)

★ Create a book called I*M*A*G*I*N*A*T*I*O*N*. First, brainstorm a list of things that imagination is. Use your list to help you decide how to make your book and what to put in it.

★ Draw a picture of your imagination.

★ Brainstorm and enter in your journal: Things you need imagination for.

★ In a small group, discuss whether or not "dragons are too seldom" in YOUR life.

★ One of my best fantasies . . . . tell someone — listen to his/her story too.

★ Some things that could use a little imagination . . . . make a list.

★ Pretend you are selling "imagination" to the public. Create an advertisement for "fantasy." Present it to your class.

★ When you say "let's pretend," what do you mean? Ask several people.

★ Keep track of your fantasies or daydreams for the next two weeks. After that time, re-read them to find any patterns in them. What do they say about you?

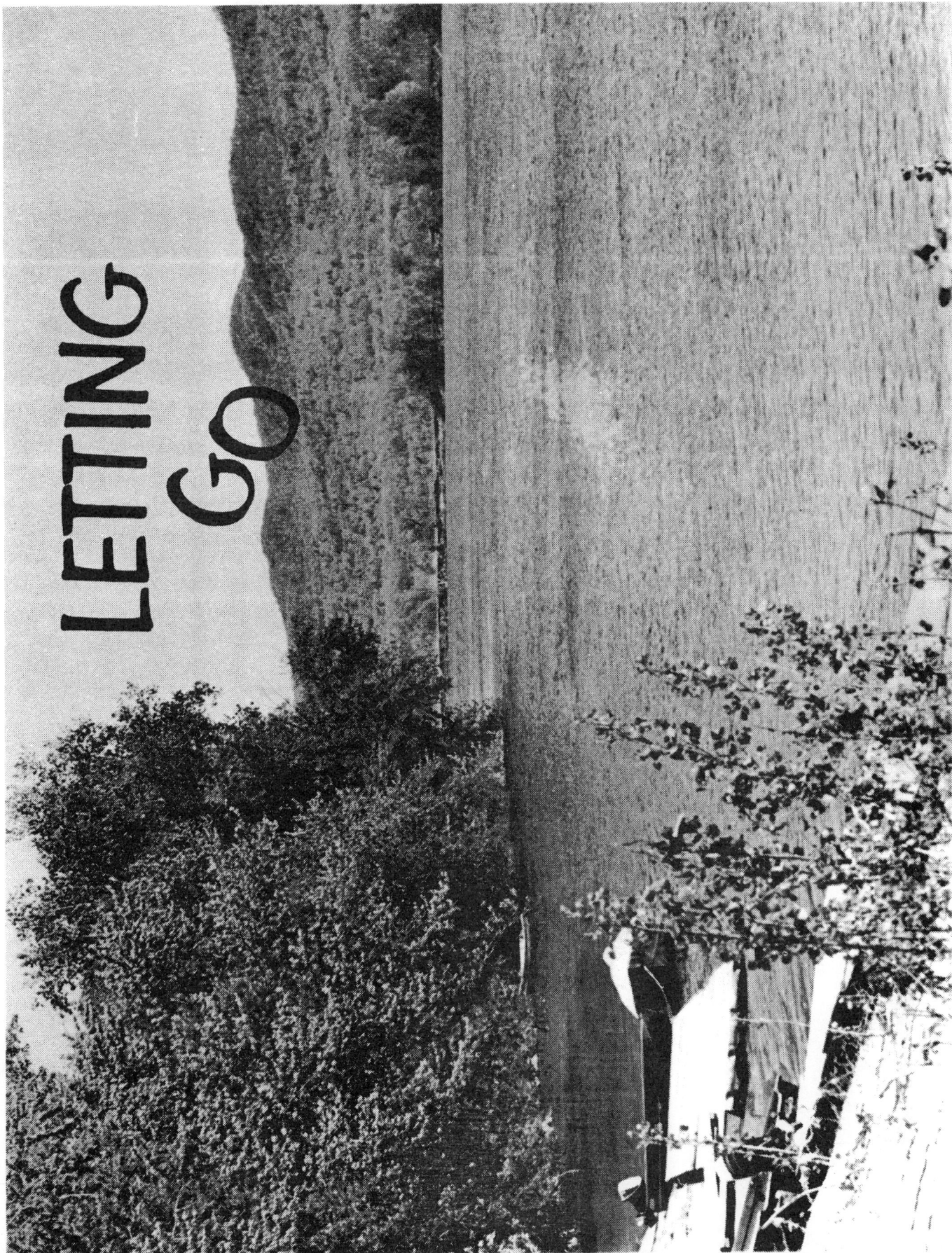

LETTING GO

"Don't push the river, it flows by itself." **F. Perls**

● With 1 or 2 other people, BRAINSTORM: "How to be patient."

● Write a poem called, "SO WHAT?"

● In a group discuss: It's easier to swim WITH the current than AGAINST it
There's nothing I can do about it anyway!
How do you know when to "let things be?"
There's a time for EVERYTHING

● Draw a picture of fate.

● List 5 words that describe the things you do whenever you are impatient.

● What would it be like to be able to MAKE something happen? Close your eyes for a moment and let yourself pretend to have that power. Zoom in on what you would do. Write about your experience in your journal.

an important message

✱ AN IMPORTANT MESSAGE ◀

"It is more important to be human than it is to be important."

▷ With 2 others, brainstorm a list of qualities that are important for people to have.

▷ As a project, take a survey and ask people to name "any important person." Graph the results. Write one or two sentences about what you discovered.

▷ An important thing to remember about being important . . . create a poster or bumper sticker with your message.

▷ In your journal, write: The most "human" person I know . . . . because . . . .
Reasons why I think I'm important

▷ As a class, discuss: Why all people are important
What it is about humans that make them important

▷ With six others, do a circletime on the topics — —
How I am important to others
A time I felt too important

important!

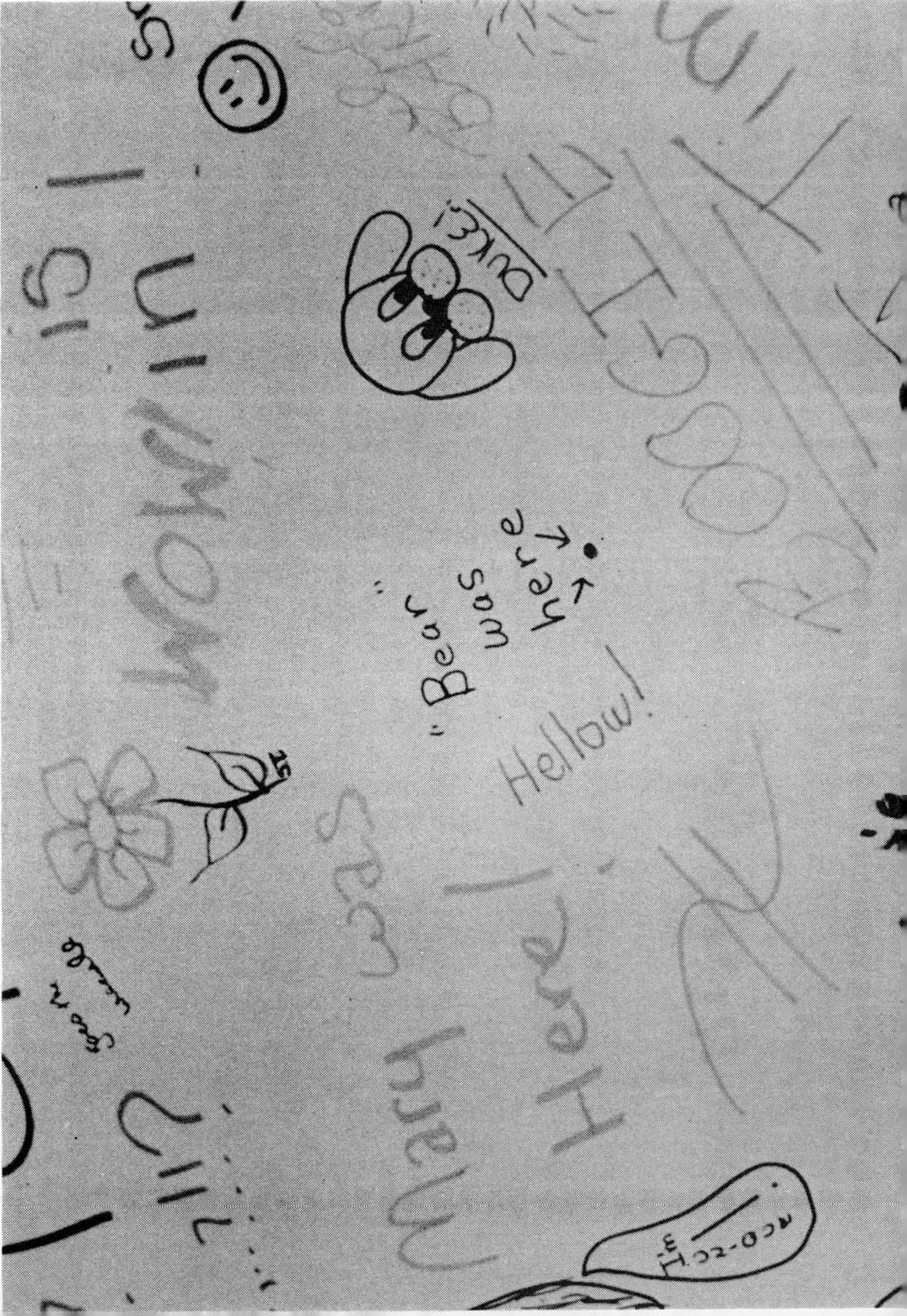

YOU DON'T SAY!

YOU DON'T SAY

"What a good thing Adam had — when he said a good thing he knew nobody had said it before." **Mark Twain**

- "You are what you say" — ARE YOU?? Explain in your journal.

- Get a large sheet of paper and make your own WALL. Use it for graffiti (have other people write on it too).

- Write 6 proverbs of your own — choose from the following topics: loyalty/ school/ money/ music/ disappointment/ children/ creativity/ television/ love/ individuality/ art/ laughter/ _____.

- Design some billboards to "advertise" quotations or proverbs you really like.

- Ask someone the question: what makes proverbs worth listening to?

- Find 1 or 2 other people; compose, rehearse and present to the class, a skit entitled: THE FIRST PROVERB.

- Write one sentence that tells something you wish you had said . . .

- Discuss in a group: *Quality* vs. *quality* of speech
  A successful proverb is one that _____ ?

say what?

A LOOK IN THE MIRROR

"If I shall be like him, who shall be like me?" Jewish Proverb.

■ In your journal, brainstorm: WHO ARE YOU? Keep asking yourself this question.

■ In what ways do you try to be like other people? List.

■ Agree to exchange personalities with someone. Spend some time being them and them you. Watch *how* they are you. What do they do to be you? See what you can learn about how people see you (remember what you are looking at isn't you). Answer this question: CAN YOU BE SOMEONE ELSE? Discuss with your partner.

■ Class discussion: How to devise a plan to prevent you from becoming extinct
Somewhere in the world you have a twin
A copy is as good as the real thing
What trying to be like other people gets for you/cost you

■ Write a poem called "I Am What I Am (And That's All I Ever Can Be)."

■ Get with a partner and take 2 minutes asking each other these questions:
When do you pretend?
What do you want?
Who are you?
How is this like looking in a mirror?

TAKE A .... PICTURE

"It is difficult to see the picture when you are inside the frame." **R.S. Trapp**

■ List 5 words that describe the way you act when you are *involved*.

■ When people say, "I'm really *into this*," they mean _____

■ Make a collage or chart to show the things you are really involved in.

■ Close your eyes for a few moments and get outside of your "frame." What do you see? Enter this information in your journal.

■ In a small group, discuss:

When it is necessary for a person to step out of his/her frame
What makes it difficult for people to be objective?
Ways to remove yourself from a situation (or experience)

■ What is your "frame of reference?" Draw a picture of it.

■ In a letter to yourself, explain which is harder for you: looking out OR looking in.

■ Find out what the difference is between an OBJECTIVE opinion and a SUBJECTIVE opinion. Tell someone about the difference.

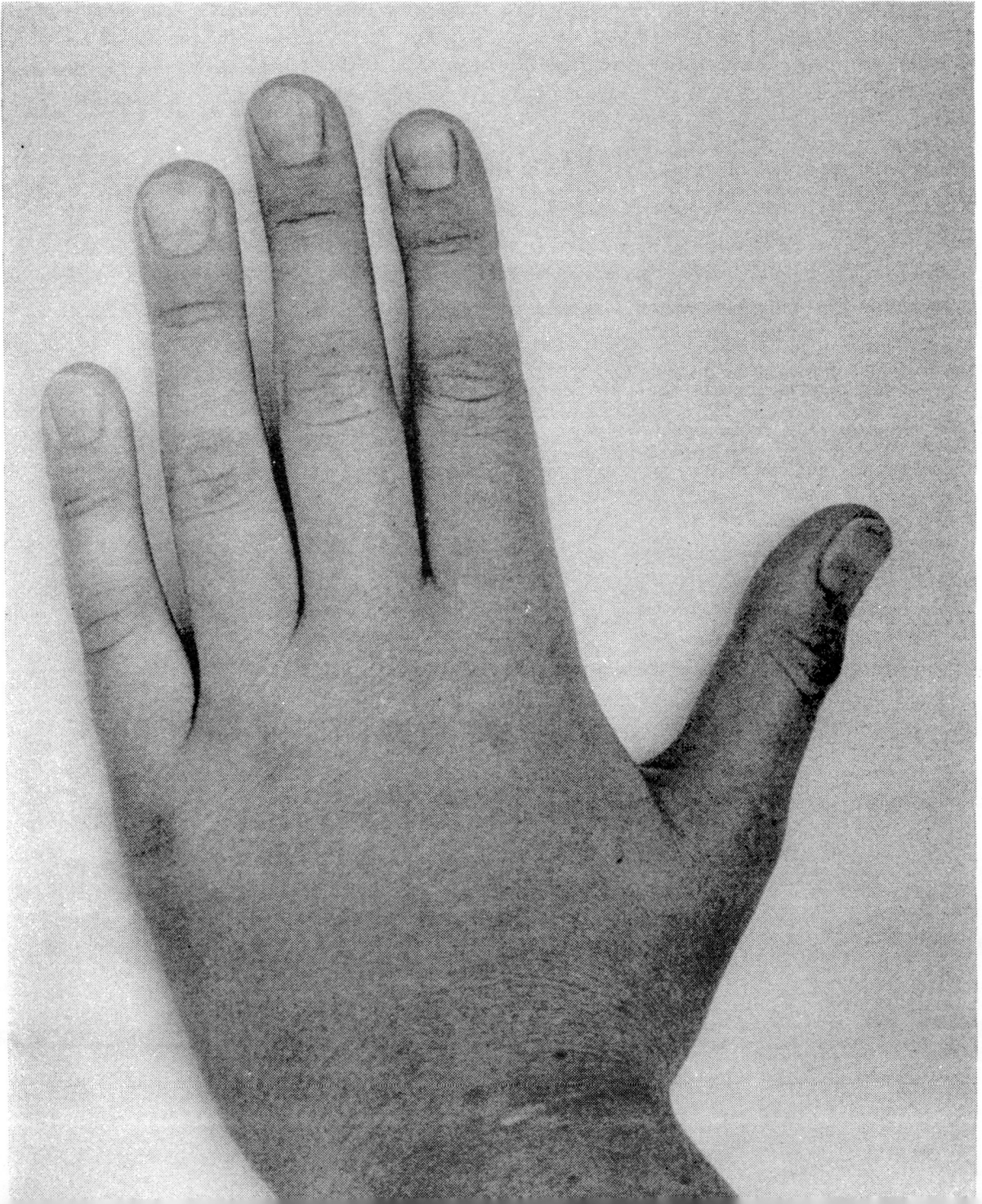

59

HELP!!!

"The best place to find a helping hand is at the end of your arm." Elmer Leterman

---

☐ How much help do you need in a day? Keep a record of the times you NEED help — write what the problem is, who you want help from, if you ask for help, if you get it, and how the problem is solved (or why it isn't). When you finish, write a paragraph in your journal about yourself out of this experience.

☐ Brainstorm with one or two other people: "Ways of Helping." Make a chart with this information.

☐ Fill in the blank: One thing I really need help with is _____

☐ List 5 words that describe the way you act when you help someone.

☐ Write yourself a reminder about a time you helped yourself.

☐ Discuss in a group: Most of the time when people get help they don't need it
        Is help ever wasted?
        How you know when you need help

☐ With your sharing-partner-for-the-day, practice ways of asking for help.

☐ In your journal, write about whether it is harder for you to help yourself
        OR
        other people.

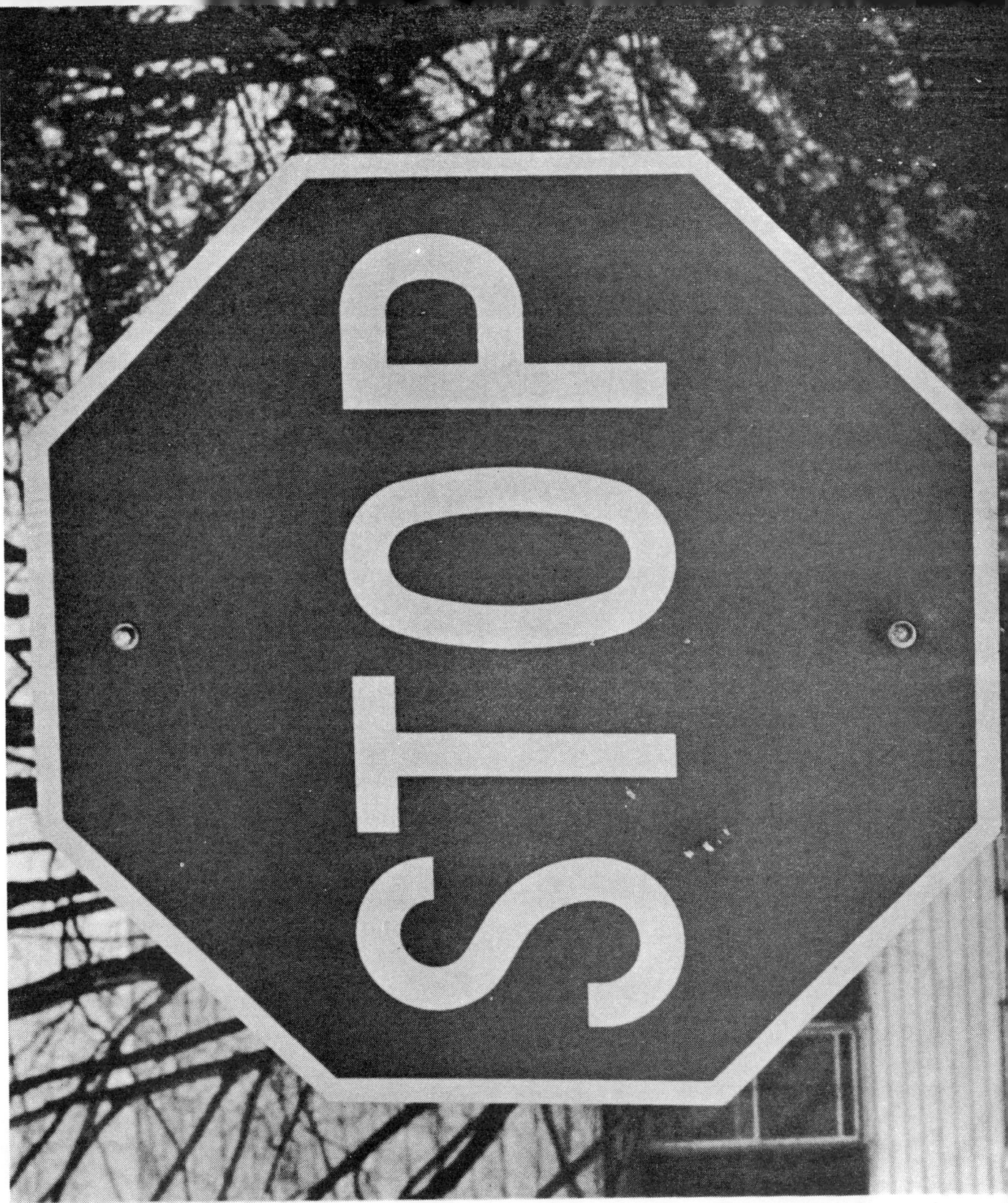

WHO QUIES?

WHO RULES?

60

"Rules are for when brains run out." George Papashvily

- Brainstorm with one or two others, some rules you *don't* need because you'd know what to do anyway.

- In your journal, write how you "know" what to do, what to say, and how to act.

- Class discussions: How do people "get" common sense?
  What if you only had instincts?
  How rules make you dependent
  How is having no rules, the rule?

- In a small group, brainstorm: Rules you wish you had
  Ways to rule with no rules

the

rule

is...

- Close your eyes: "see" your school without rules. What is happening? Share this experience with one or two others.

- How would you act differently if there were NO rules? Write a paragraph in your journal.

- Keep a record for a week of ALL rules that you follow. Divide your list into rules that are self-created and rules that are other-created. Also, write the reason (if you know it) for the rule. At the end of the week, review your lists and discuss, with one or two others, what you found out about yourself from this experience.

PLAYING WITH BLOCKS

PLAYING WITH BLOCKS

"People are lonely because they build walls instead of bridges." J. F. Newton

● "Words are the bridges we build to reach each other." Write a poem or make a collage using some of these words.

● Brainstorm with a partner: Ways to "Build Bridges."

● What is loneliness? In a circle, tell about a time YOU experienced being lonely.

● Make a list of clues that tell you when a person is lonely.

● Write 1 sentence that tells how loneliness touches you.

● In a group, discuss: Is loneliness self-created or other-created?
   How to tear down walls.
   The difference between being ALONE and LONELY.

● A lonely place/ A lonely time/ A lonely sound/ A lonely idea/ A lonely experience . . . choose 3 of these to share with someone. Listen to his/her story too.

● In your journal, write about: "A bridge I've Built — A wall I've built . . . and what they've gotten for me."

blocks

IT'S A JOKE

IT'S A JOKE !!!

"Laughter is the shortest distance between two people." **Victor Borge**

hA

■ Class discussions: How can laughter bring people closer together?
How can it make people feel far apart?
What if we couldn't laugh?
Do animals laugh?

ha

■ Make a JOKE BOOK — write down your favorite jokes and/or funny stories, and ask other people for theirs'. Illustrate, and combine into a book to share with your class.

■ Brainstorm with a group:
· All the things we have around us that try to make us laugh
· The things people laugh at most
· The purposes of laughter
· Ways to make people laugh

ha

HA

■ Individual Project: For one day, keep a log on what people laugh about.

■ Class Project: Record the different laughs in your class. How are they the same or different?

■ Write a song, poem, or story designed to make people laugh. Share it with your classmates.

■ Where does laughter start? Where does it go? Draw a map that traces its path.

ha

YOUR TWO ② FACES

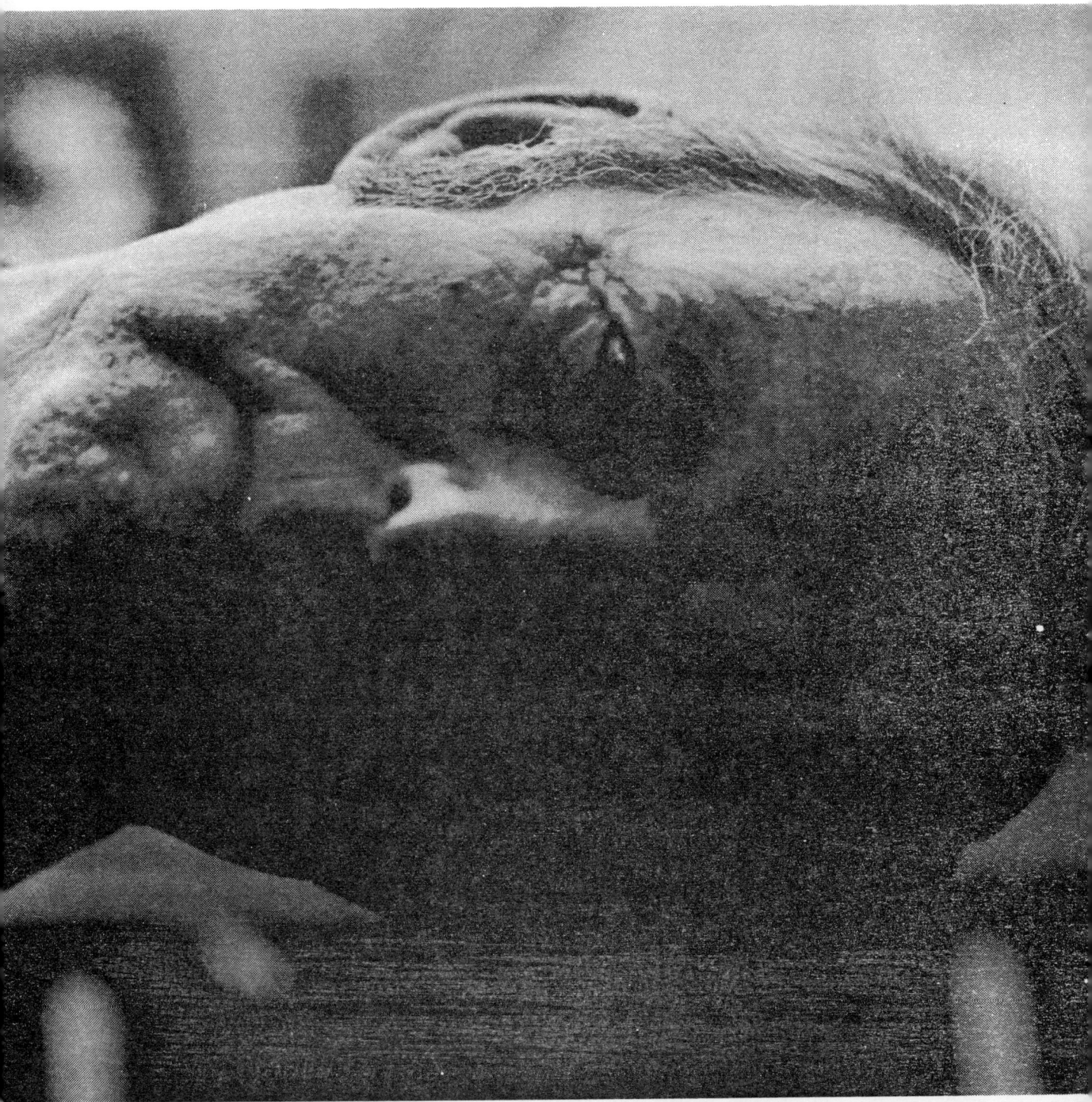

"Everyone is a moon and has a dark side which he never shows anybody." **Mark Twain**

- Make a graph to show how much of you is kept hidden away.

- In your mind, describe to yourself the KINDS of things you keep to yourself. Write some of this information in your journal.

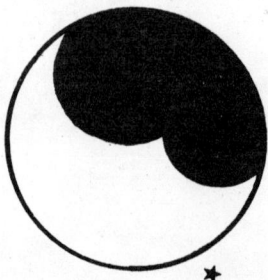

- Write one sentence that tells about privacy.

- In a note, write down a little known fact about you that might surprise someone. Give it to that someone.

- List **5** words that describe the things you do whenever you want privacy.

- Write a story or poem about your secret life.

- Close your eyes for a moment and think of yourself as having two lives — public (outer) and private (inner) . . . tell someone how your two lives blend together to make you.

- Write yourself a letter about what you think might happen if people found out about your "other" side.

- Fill in the blank: What keeps me from "showing" people certain things about me is _____ .

CHASING RAINBOWS

"We all live under the same sky, but we don't all have the same horizon." Konrad Adenauer

• In your journal, make a list of the goals you have. In what way is this your horizon?

• What is YOUR "pot of gold?" Draw a picture.

SOMEWHERE—?

• Write a letter to yourself that you will open in one month — write about where you hope to be, what you want to be doing, things you want to have settled, where you'd like your head to be at, etc. . . . Put your letter in a safe place and open it in one month!

• Interview some people (at least 10) about their ambitions. Make a list of the different goals and write one or two sentences about what you learned.

• Pick out one of your goals and do something TODAY to help make it happen. In your journal, write about the course of action you take.

• Some people think that when you set goals you should be realistic. Others say be idealistic . . . if you are realistic, you won't be disappointed; if you are idealistic, you'll go further than you thought. Have a class discussion on this topic. Get opinions from people outside your class.

• Ideas on what you want to do with your life come from many places. In your journal, list some of these places.

INSIDE & OUT

"What really matters is what happens in us, not to us." **Rev. James W. Kennedy**

- In your journal: make a list of things that happen INSIDE of you and another list of things that happen TO you. Compare, and write one or two sentences about what you find out.

- Write a poem or make a collage about the "happenings" in your life.

- In a small group, discuss: *"I cannot* control the circumstances of my situation, I can only experience my experience of it."

- Outside growth in people is usually seen in inches (feet) and pounds. Inside growth is harder to "see." Have a class brainstorm on: ways people grow from the inside. With a partner, brainstorm a list of how to make things happen.

- Close your eyes and see yourself (and other people) growing up "inside-out." (Feelings on the outside). Stay "there" for 2 or 3 minutes. How would this reversal change people and their relationships? Share your thoughts with someone.

SEEING RED

"People who fly into a rage always make a bad landing." **Will Rogers**

Draw a picture of YOUR temper.

Make an "anger collage." (Ideas: ANGRY colors/words/foods/things in nature/places . . . .)

Fill in the blanks: AFTER I lose my temper, I ————
.I show I'm angry by ————
My anger gets me ————

Brainstorm with a partner a list of things to do INSTEAD of losing your temper. Make a chart and share with the class.

Write 1 or 2 sentences that tell about a time you experienced anger.

In your journal, write about: WHEN you feel yourself losing control (in what situations).

With your sharing-partner-for-the-day, discuss: When you "lose control," what do you lose?

Close your eyes for a moment and "play-back" a time you felt VERY angry. What was it like to be that angry? Enter this information in your journal.

Write a poem about things that anger you. Share it with someone.

WHEN YOU CARE ENOUGH

"No act of kindness, no matter how small, is ever wasted."

⊙ Write a recipe for kindness.

⊙ Design your own line of "Thoughtfulness Greeting Cards." Send them out.

⊙ Start a "Be Kind To ——— Day." Make plans (for how to) and BEGIN!

how NICE!

⊙ Fill in the blanks: Someone was kind to me when ———
In return for MY kindness I expect to receive ———.

⊙ Write a reminder to yourself about the things you'd like to do for other people.

⊙ Ask some people the question: What causes you to care? Ask yourself too.

⊙ Close your eyes and remember a time when you did something nice for someone. Notice everything about it. How do you feel? What is the experience? Enter this information in your journal. Tell your sharing-partner-for-the-day and listen to his/her story too.

⊙ Trace a cartoon but leave the word balloons blank. Fill in the dialogue yourself. TOPIC: Kindness.

DID you EVER have TO make UP your MIND?

DID YOU EVER HAVE TO MAKE UP YOUR MIND?

"When you have to make a choice and you don't make it, that in itself is a choice." **William James**

• In your journal, list things that you are able to choose for yourself. Make another list of things other people choose for you. Compare your lists and write 1 or 2 sentences about what you found out.

• As a class, discuss: "Choosing is existence (life). If you don't choose, you don't exist." Which is worse — making a wrong decision OR not making a decision at all?

• Draw a picture of INDECISION.   either... or?

• If you don't make a decision, what happens? Brainstorm a list of possibilities with one or two other people.

• MAKE A DECISION — Tape or write your answers in your journal (explain your choice if you can):

1. Two people are drowning. If you act immediately you can save one of them. No one else is around. You do not know either of the people. One is an adult, one is a child. Who will you save?

2. Which came first — the chicken OR the egg?

3. It is up to you to choose the first U.S. citizen to travel to Mars. You may pick anyone you want (other than yourself), famous or non-famous. This is an extremely great honor for the person you pick and the whole country is waiting to hear your decision . . . who will you choose?

4. You have just been given $10 to spend anyway you want. You really need a pair of jeans, but you also what to buy some record albums and go to the movies with your friends very much. There is no other way for you to get the money for any of the these things. What will you spend the money on?

• Fill in the blanks: A time I changed my mind _____.
A decision I found easy to make _____.
A decision I found hard to make _____.

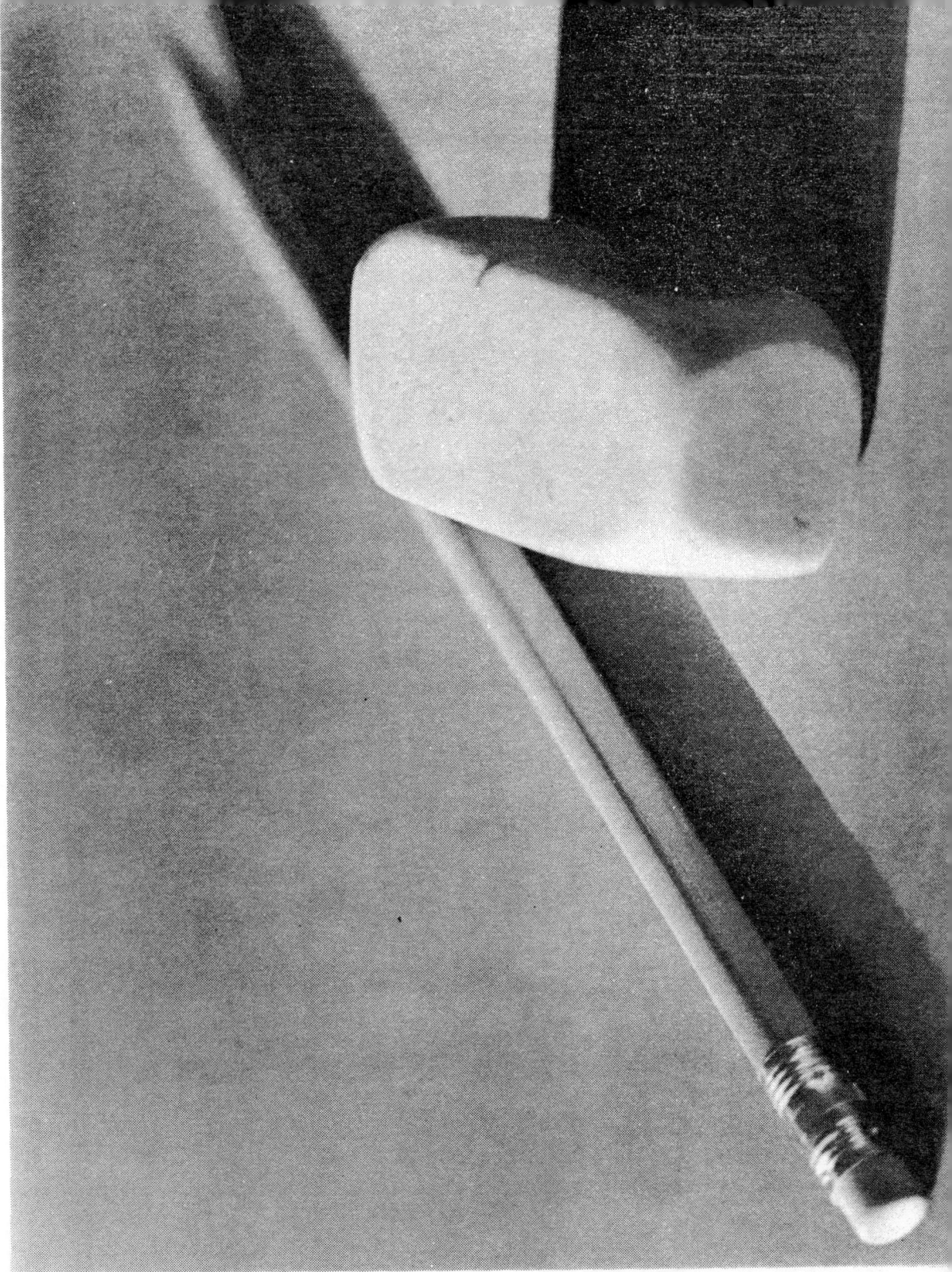

SHARPPEN YOUR PENCIL

"Life is the art of drawing without an eraser." John Christian

Get a piece of paper and a pencil and draw at least 3 things in your classroom. Focus your attention on each one and notice everything about it. Do NOT use your eraser — even once! Do NOT get another piece of paper — even if you make a mistake. When you finish, (in your journal) describe how you felt while you were drawing and what you learned by doing it this way. ●

Make a list to answer this question: If you can't erase things that happen, what can you do instead? ●

Make a chart that shows: How To Avoid Making Mistakes. Share with your class. ●

Ask some people the question: "How do you know when you've made a mistake?" ●

With one or two other people discuss: "There's always time to add a word, never to withdraw one." Why do mistakes happen? Are mistakes cause or effect? ●

List 5 words that describe the way you feel about making a mistake. ●

Write yourself a short note about how your mistakes can work for you. ●

Explain to someone: why erasers *don't really* work OR how they *really* work. ●

What does a mistake show? In your journal, list at least 3 different things. ●

WHOOPS

A LESSON IN LOVE

"We like because, we love despite."

• With another person, illustrate the difference between "liking" and "loving." How will you know others know what you mean?

• Class discussion: If the whole world would fall in love — what would happen to hate?
Why is love "DESPITE?"
What do the following have to do with love:

• tolerance
• intimacy
• romance
• trust
• sharing
• security
• obligation

• A person I love . . . a place I love . . . a thing I love. Write a "love poem" about each.

• Write a story to explain how and why the heart became a symbol of love.

• Design a "new" symbol for love.

• Do some whips on:

I know I love someone when _____
When I like someone I _____
When I love someone I _____

hearing THINGS

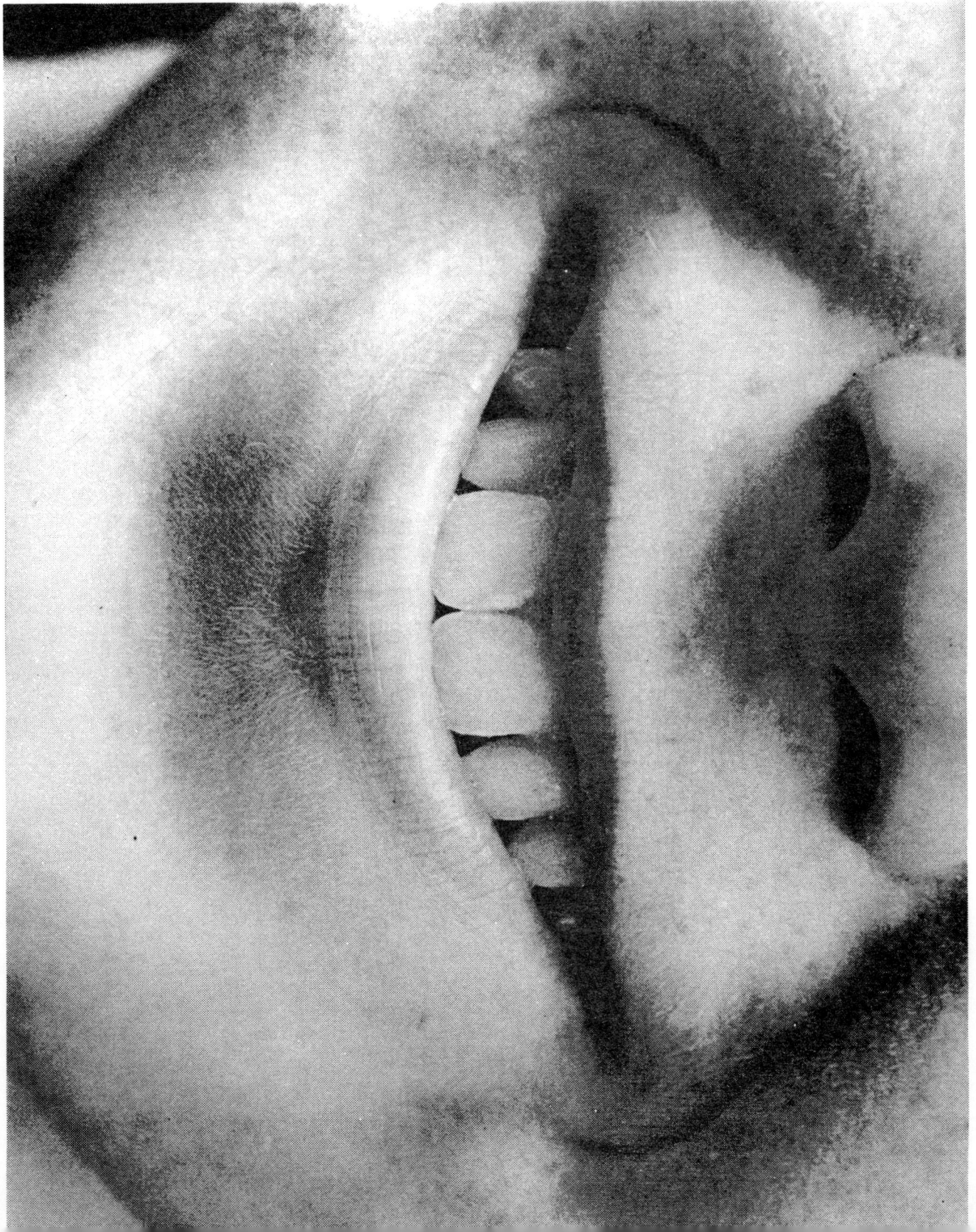

"If you do not understand my silence, you will not understand my words."

SILENCE . . .

● Write a poem describing the sound(s) of silence.

● As a class, be silent for one hour (or more). When the time is up, in your journal, write about how you felt during this experience and what you found easy and/or hard about about keeping quiet.

● Brainstorm with another person: Imagine that when you wake up tomorrow, you will be living in a world *totally without sounds.* Make a list of all the sounds you will miss.

● In a small group, listen to some records of sound effects. Make your own "record" by taping sounds. Have people listen and guess what sounds you've taped.

● Listen to the pauses between people's words and sentences — listen between the words, rather than to the words. What can be learned from these "spaces?" Discuss with your sharing-partner-for-the-day.

● Do some whips on:

    Times I am silent I am usually _____ .

    Silence says _____ .

    Silence is _____ .

● Alone activity: Listen to the warm . . . listen to a rainbow . . . listen to purple . . . listen to jello . . . listen to cotton . . . listen to the moonlight . . . Pick three and illustrate or describe their sounds.

Do YOU see what I see?

"People only see what they are prepared to see." **Emerson**

● A lot of "seeing" depends on close *observation.* Choose 3 of the following to observe and write about: The difference between your right hand and your left hand/ one strand of your hair/ the door to your classroom/ a fingernail/ a line made by a pencil/ glass . . . . . .

● With your sharing-partner-for-the-day, try answering these questions using your memory:
  does the front door of your school swing in or out?
  how many windows are in your house?
  which letters are missing on a telephone dial?
  which side is the hot water on?
  what is the lowest number on the AM radio dial?
  what color are your teacher's eyes?
  whose picture is on the quarter?

*noW you see it. . .
noW you don't!*

● Brainstorm a list of things that could influence what you see.

● Write 1 word (or sentence) that describes the difference between "looking" and "seeing"

● In a group, discuss: Is it possible to see EXACTLY what other people see?
  When you say, "I see," what do you mean?

● Something I thought I saw, but didn't . . . . write about it in your journal.

● Right now, put ALL of your attention on _____ **?** Write about or illustrate what you see.

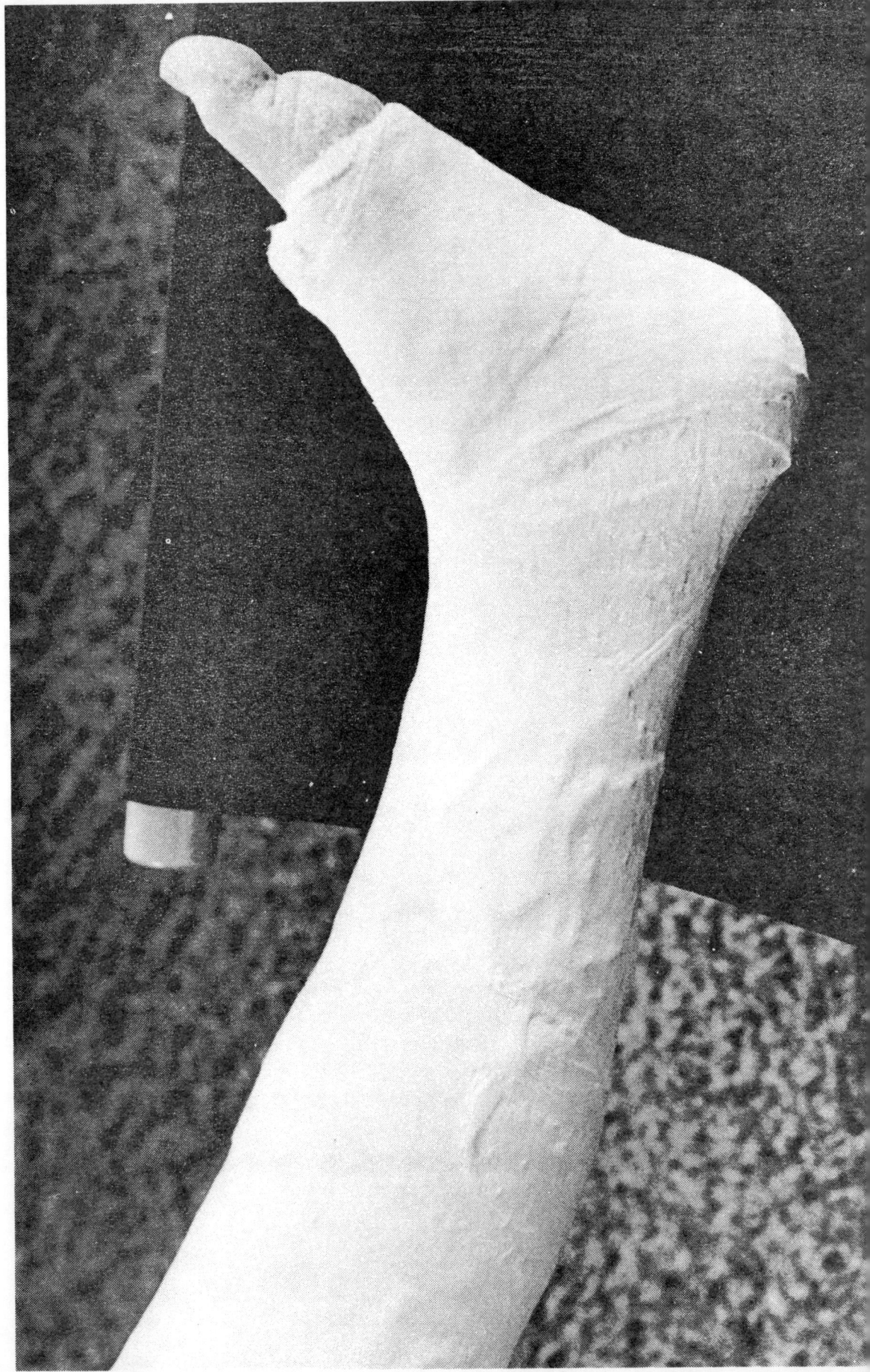

GETTING BY

GETTING BY . . .

"Although the world is full of suffering, it is full also of the overcoming of it." Helen Keller

GETTING OVER IT . . .

■ Ask some people: How do things "get better?" Compare their answers with yours.

■ Write three things you say to yourself when things aren't going well for you.

■ Journal entry: Something I got over (and how I did it) . . . .

■ In a small group, discuss: "Time heals all wounds." Everything that happens, happens for a reason

■ Make up a dictionary entry for: "rolling with the punches."

■ Write a poem about "old hurts."

■ If life gives you _____ ? _____ make _____ ? _____ . Fill in the blanks and design a poster.

■ When your hurt goes away, where does it go? Discuss with your sharing-partner-for-the-day.

REVOLVING QUESTIONS

"Just when I thought I knew all of the answer, they changed all of the questions."

➤ In a group, discuss: How do you know what you know?
How do you know what you don't know?
What's worth knowing?
"Strange how much you've got to know before you know how little you know" (Duncan Stuart)

➤ Brainstorm a list of things that you now know. Write this list in your journal.

➤ Close your eyes and "see" yourself — making a phone call
crossing the street
caring for a plant
talking to a person you just met
spending money

➤ What do you need to know in order to do these things? Discuss with your sharing-partner-for-the-day.

➤ Fill in the blank: If only I had known _____

➤ Close your eyes and "see" yourself as a very young child. Let yourself pretend to be a baby for a few minutes. As a baby, what advice would you like people to give you about "making it" in this world? Make a list of advice for yourself.

➤ In your journal, wirte about: why the questions keep changing? Who (or what) changes them?

IN FAVOR OF KIDS

> "*Children are our most valuable resource.*" Herbert Hoover

O **Fill in the blanks:** When I feel like a kid _____ :
When I feel older _____ :

O Brainstorm with one or two others: What's great about being a child?

O In your journal, write about some things you wish adults would remember. . . .

O In a group, discuss: — How you know when you're grown-up
— Besides ages, what are the differences between kids and adults?
— How can you find out what it feels like to be an adult?
— "We have not passed the subtle line between childhood and adulthood until we move from the passive voice to the active voice — that is, until we have stopped saying, 'It got lost,' and say, 'I lost it'." (Sidney J. Harris)

O Things that scare me about growing up — write a poem.

KIDS

O Interview some kids to find out what laws could be made to protect kids better. Choose a way to present this information to the class.

75

Beginnings

ENDINGS

AND

BEGINNINGS AND ENDINGS . . . .

"Fear not that your life shall come to an end, but rather fear that it shall never have a beginning."

- In a group, discuss: The minute you were born, you started to die
  Does life always begin when you are born?
  There are no beginnings and endings — there just "is"

- List 5 words that describe how it feels to be alive.

- In your journal, write a paragraph about things you want to do before you die.

- Circletime topics:

  Something I wonder about living . . .
  Something I wonder about death . . . .
  Living is . . . .

- In your journal, make a list of the scary and not scary things about being alive.

- Make a collage of "Things I want for myself in my lifetime."

- With your sharing-partner-for-the-day, discuss the responsibilities that you have because you are alive in the HERE and NOW.

- With a partner, brainstorm a list of ways to grow up alive.

the
circle
game

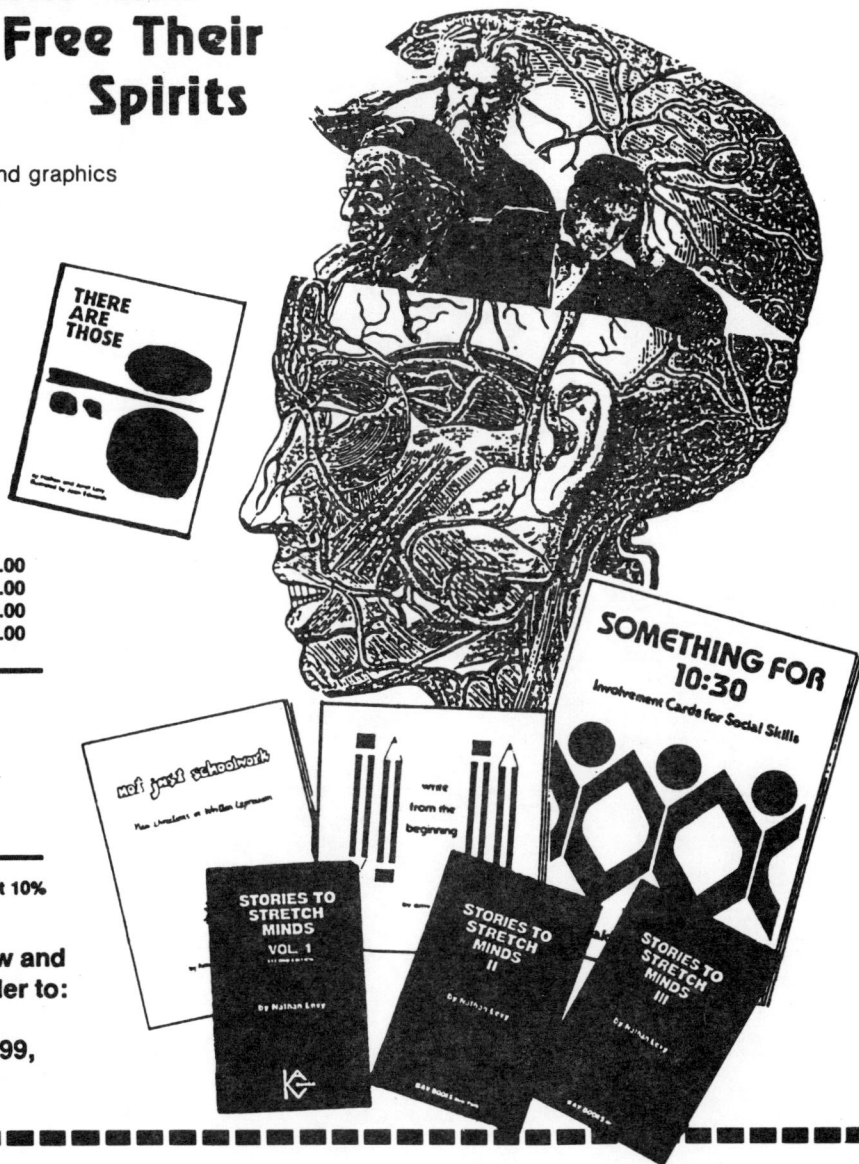